LINDA SONNTAG

MICROWAVE

COOKING

the apple press

LINDA SONNTAG
MICROWAVE
COOKING

CONTENTS

A QUINTET BOOK

Published by Apple Press Ltd
293 Gray's Inn Road
London WC1X 8QF

Copyright © 1984 Quintet
Publishing Limited
All rights reserved. No part of this
publication may be reproduced,
stored in a retrieval system, or
transmitted, in any form or by any
means, electronic, mechanical,
photocopying, recording or
otherwise, without the permission
of the copyright holder.

ISBN 1 85076 018 7

The Publishers wish to thank
Zanussi for the use of their
microwave oven in the preparation
of all the dishes in this book.
The Publishers also wish to thank
Tower Housewares,
Wolverhampton, and Pyrex-
Corning Microware, London, for
supplying the kitchenware used in
this book.

This book was designed and
produced by Quintet Publishing
Limited 32 Kingly Court,
London W1

Art Design Bridgewater Associates
Illustrator Lorraine Harrison
Photographer John Heseltine
Cookery Consultant Myra Street
Editor Cheen Horn

Typeset by Context Typesetting,
Brighton
Colour Origination in Hong Kong
by Hong Kong Graphic Arts
Limited
Printed in Hong Kong by Leefung-
Asco Printers Limited

The microwave oven makes cooking a pleasure. It is a sophisticated appliance that is extremely simple to use. It is economical, hygienic – and extremely fast. For the busy cook it is an invaluable asset, especially when used in combination with a freezer.

In a matter of minutes it produces delicious food that has lost none of its fresh flavour or nutritional value. And it minimizes washing up. Cooking with the microwave keeps your kitchen cool and free of steam and food odours. It is so safe that children and disabled people can operate it easily – and its control panels can even be translated into braille for the blind.

Conventional cooking takes place when heat is applied to the outside of food – it takes a while to penetrate the middle. Microwaves vibrate the molecules of the food in the oven, creating heat that cooks the food quickly because it affects the inside of the food at the same time as the outside. This means that the food shrinks less and keeps its fresh colour and succulent taste.

GETTING THE BEST OUT OF YOUR MICROWAVE
Utensils

1 Browning dishes are an invaluable aid for searing meat, and special microwave browning agents are also available. Microwave roasting racks allow the juices to run from meat and poultry while cooking.
2 You can use virtually any kitchenware or china in your microwave oven, but don't use metal containers in it. Don't use dishes decorated with silver or gold. The microwaves bounce off the metal and can damage your oven. Avoid plastic containers, which may warp, and melamine, which becomes pitted.

3 If you are unsure of the suitability of a container for microwave cookery, you can test it by putting it into the oven next to a glass half-filled with water. Turn on the oven for 1 minute. If the dish is hotter than the water, then it would not be wise to use it.
4 Remember not to leave a meat thermometer in meat while cooking.

Preparation

1 Cut foods to approximately the same size where possible, and spread them out in a single layer to cook.
2 Arrange foods in a circle where possible, with the thinner part of the food towards the centre.
3 Arrange fish head to tail in a dish.
4 Cover narrow ends of meat, such as tips of chicken wings, and heads and tails of fish with foil to avoid overcooking.
5 Remember that foods of lower temperature take longer to cook, so add a fraction extra time for refrigerated foods.
6 Always cover foods when reheating.

Special Microwave Dishes

Cooking

1 Quantity of food and cooking time are roughly proportional. When cooking twice the quantity, the time required may be a little less than double.

2 Remember that smaller or thinner pieces of food will cook quicker than larger or fatter pieces.

3 Irregular items should be turned or rearranged in the dish during cooking.

4 Don't deep fry or use batter.

5 Don't attempt to boil eggs in the microwave – they may explode.

6 Always prick the yolk of an egg before poaching.

7 Cheese cooks very quickly in the microwave. Overcooking will make it tough and rubbery.

8 Irregular items should be turned or rearranged in the dish during cooking.

9 Add foods that cook faster towards the end of cooking time. For example, if you are making a meat casserole with peas, add the peas just before cooking is completed.

10 Don't overtime – reheating is very quick and successful because foods don't dry out, they retain their colour, texture, flavour and nutrients.

Hot tips

1 To heat baby food, remove the metal top from the jar, cover loosely with cling film and microwave for approximately 1 minute. Test temperature.

2 You can make beverages such as instant coffee, chocolate or hot toddy cheaply and conveniently in the microwave. Place the ingredients in a cup and heat for 1 – 2 minutes on full. Stir well before drinking.

3 Save electricity and washing up by using your microwave to melt jellies, gelatine, cooking chocolate and butter in the dish you are going to cook in.

4 Use a low power setting for ripening Brie and other cheeses, and a warm setting for softening frozen ice cream.

5 Bring stale rolls back to life by wrapping in a damp cotton serviette and heating for 30 seconds on full. Eat while hot.

6 You will get more juice out of citrus fruits if you microwave them on full for 30 seconds.

7 You can dry out damp salt and sugar in the microwave, and fresh bread can be dried quickly to make breadcrumbs.

Roasting dish

Browning dish

Roasting dish

ADAPTING ORDINARY RECIPES FOR MICROWAVE COOKING

When adapting a favourite recipe for microwave cooking, follow these simple instructions:

1 Make sure your recipe is suitable for the microwave oven. If it requires, for instance, a crisp crust, you would do better to stick to conventional methods.

2 Find a similar recipe in your microwave cook book. Note the technique and recommended timing. If the quantities of both recipes are similar, techniques and timing will be much the same.

3 Microwaving should take roughly a quarter of conventional cooking time. Begin with this and add more if necessary.

4 Use larger dishes than with conventional cooking to avoid food boiling over.

5 Reduce the liquid in your recipe by a quarter as liquid does not evaporate during microwave cooking to the same extent as in conventional cooking.

6 Microwaving retains the flavour of the food better than conventional cooking, so use less seasoning and season again after cooking if necessary.

7 If you are using rice or noodles in the recipe, choose the quick-cooking variety to avoid over-cooking the rest of the ingredients before the rice or noodles are done.

Vegetables

Microwave vegetables – whether fresh, frozen or canned – are a delight, because they cook perfectly while retaining their crispness, colour and natural taste. Hardly any nutrients are lost, since only 2 – 3 tbs water are needed per 450 g / 1 lb vegetables.

Always cover vegetables with cling film and slit in 2 or 3 places before cooking, or use a dish with a lid. If heating frozen vegetables, place the bag in a dish and pierce. Vegetables being cooked in their skins, such as potatoes, do not need water, but should be pricked to prevent exploding. Canned vegetables should be drained, placed in a dish with a lid or slit cling film to cover and cooked for 2 – 3 minutes per 425 g / 15 oz can.

Always arrange large or uneven pieces, such as broccoli spears, with the tenderer parts towards the centre of the oven, and turn the dish once during cooking. Whole bulky vegetables, such as a cauliflower, should be turned over half way through the cooking time. Smaller vegetables should be stirred once, and packets of frozen vegetables shaken to redistribute the contents.

The age and thickness of vegetables will affect cooking time, and personal tastes vary too, so make regular checks while the vegetables are in the oven, using the table below as a guide, to avoid overcooking. Remember that after the vegetables have been removed from the oven they will continue to cook for a couple of minutes because of the heat retained within them.

Season vegetables after they have been cooked. Salt sprinkled on top of vegetables before cooking causes toughening of the skins and gives a dried-out darkened appearance.

Dried pulses should be soaked overnight in cold water before cooking, or microwaved and allowed to stand for 1 – 1½ hours to swell and soften. To cook, place pulses in a large container and cover with boiling water. Smaller pulses, such as lentils, will need 20 – 25 minutes, and larger ones 40 – 60 minutes. Cover while cooking and top up the water if necessary.

Blanching vegetables in the microwave for freezing saves a kitchen full of steam. Prepare the vegetables in the normal way and place them in a large casserole with about 5 – 6 tbs water per 450 g / 1 lb. Cook vegetables for half the time recommended in the chart, stirring or rearranging once. Cool by plunging into iced water, pack and freeze in the normal way. When defrosted, cook for the same amount of time as fresh vegetables. If cooking from the freezer, allow an extra 1 – 3 minutes.

Drying herbs is a simple, quick and clean process in the microwave. Arrange them between layers of absorbent kitchen paper and cook until the leaves can be crumbled. Store in dark glass jars out of the reach of sunlight to prevent fading.

FRESH VEGETABLES/COOKING GUIDE

vegetables	quantity	minutes on full
artichokes	4	10 – 20
asparagus	225 g / 8 oz	6 – 7
aubergines, diced	450 g / 1 lb	5 – 6
beans, broad, french or runner	450 g / 1 lb	8 – 10
beetroot, sliced	450 g / 1 lb	7 – 8
broccoli	450 g / 1 lb	4 – 5
Brussels sprouts	450 g / 1 lb	8 – 10
cabbage	450 g / 1 lb	7 – 10
carrots	225 g / 8 oz	7 – 10
cauliflower florets	450 g / 1 lb	10 – 11
celery	1 head	10 – 13
corn on the cob	1	3 – 5
courgettes, sliced	450 g / 1 lb	7 – 10
leeks, sliced	450 g / 1 lb	7 – 10
marrow, sliced	450 g / 1 lb	8 – 10
mushrooms	225 g / 8 oz	5 – 6
okra	450 g / 1 lb	8 – 10
onions, sliced	225 g / 8 oz	5 – 7
parsnips, sliced	225 g / 8 oz	8 – 10
peas	450 g / 1 lb	8 – 10
potatoes, new	450 g / 1 lb	10 – 12
potatoes, jacket	2 large	9
potatoes, boiled	450 g / 1 lb	6 – 7
spinach	450 g / 1 lb	6 – 8
spring greens	450 g / 1 lb	7 – 9
swede, diced	450 g / 1 lb	6 – 7
tomatoes, sliced	225 g / 8 oz	2 – 3
turnips, diced	225 g / 8 oz	6 – 7

FROZEN VEGETABLES/COOKING GUIDE

vegetables	quantity	minutes on full
asparagus	225 g / 8 oz	6 – 7
beans, broad, french or runner	225 g / 8 oz	7
broccoli	225 g / 8 oz	6 – 8
cabbage	225 g / 8 oz	6 – 7
carrots	225 g / 8 oz	6 – 7
cauliflower	225 g / 8 oz	4 – 6
corn kernels	225 g / 8 oz	4 – 6
corn on the cob	1	4 – 5
courgettes	225 g / 8 oz	4
peas	225 g / 8 oz	4
spinach	225 g / 8 oz	7 – 8
stewpack	225 g / 8 oz	6 – 8
swedes	225 g / 8 oz	7
turnips	225 g / 8 oz	8
vegetables, mixed	225 g / 8 oz	4 – 6

FRUIT/COOKING GUIDE

fruit	quantity	minutes on full
apples	450 g / 1 lb	6 – 8
apricots	450 g / 1 lb	6 – 8
berries (any soft berry fruit)	450 g / 1 lb	3 – 5
cherries	450 g / 1 lb	3 – 5
gooseberries	450 g / 1 lb	4
peaches	4	4 – 5
pears	6	8 – 10
plums (also damsons, greengages)	450 g / 1 lb	4 – 5
rhubarb	450 g / 1 lb	7 – 10

Fruit should be prepared as for conventional cooking and sprinkled with sugar. No water is needed.

When defrosting, gently shake or stir the fruit during the process and allow to stand at room temperature afterwards until completely thawed. For 450 g / 1 lb fruit, dry packed with sugar, allow 4 – 8 minutes on full power. If fruit is packed with sugar syrup, allow 8 – 12 minutes on full. If fruit is open frozen, allow 4 – 8 minutes on defrost.

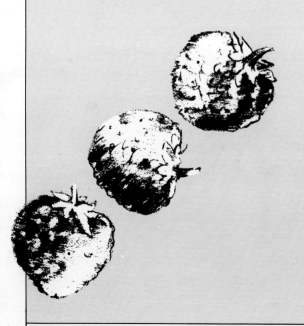

MEAT/DEFREEZING AND COOKING GUIDE

Your microwave oven will cook all types and cuts of meat in one third to half the conventional cooking time. Always remember that the meat will need to stand before serving to allow it to equalize in temperature.

A browning dish will prove most useful with meat cookery, but you can experiment too with sauces and glazes to give an appetizing appearance.

Before cooking, weigh the meat carefully. Season and place in a roasting bag on an upturned saucer, or wrap meat in greaseproof paper. Meat can also be cooked in a covered clay pot. Shield thin ends of roasts to prevent overcooking.

When cooking less tender cuts of meat, use a lower setting to give the meat time to tenderise. If your oven doesn't have a variable power setting, allow the meat to rest for regular 5 minute periods during cooking time to achieve the best results.

During cooking turn meat 4 times at regular intervals. If juices collect in the roasting bag, drain them off to accelerate cooking and prevent spitting. When cooking small cuts of meat, rearrange them during cooking time. Cook bacon and sausages on a roasting rack and cover with absorbent kitchen paper. Sausages should be pricked before cooking.

SMALL CUTS OF MEAT

meat and weight	defrost minutes	standing minutes	special points	minutes on full
mince, 450 g / 1 lb	10	2	in a dish covered with pierced cling film	5
mince, with vegetables, 450 g / 1 lb	11	10	break up after 6 minutes	5 – 6 5 – 6
steak, rump or fillet, 225 g / 8 oz	8-9	2	separate pieces during defreezing	3 – 4
braising meat, beef or lamb	10	10	in a dish covered with pierced cling film, separate pieces during defreezing	8
chops, loin, separate chops lamb or pork, 2 portions, 150 g /5 oz each	5 6	2	during defreezing	

SMALL CUTS OF MEAT				
meat and weight	defrost minutes	standing minutes	special points	minutes on full
chops, chump, lamb or pork, 2 portions, 275 g / 10 oz each	8–10	2	separate chops during defreezing; sprinkle with seasoning before cooking	7
fillet, lamb or pork, 350 g / 12 oz	7–9	5	turn during defreezing; cook covered with pierced cling film	3 on full then 12 on low
breast of lamb, 550 g / 1 lb 4 oz	7–9	3	in a large dish, covered; turn over during defreezing; cook on roasting rack sprinkled with browning agent	6
bacon, 450 g / 1 lb	6–7	2	cook on rack and separate rashers before standing time	4
chipolata sausages, 450 g / 1 lb	7–9	5	separate during defreezing	3
thick sausages	8–10	5	separate during defreezing	4
chicken, 2 portions, 425 g / 15 oz each	14–16	15, then wash	defreeze with thinnest part to centre of dish; cover thinnest part with foil, place on rack then sprinkle with browning agent to cook	10
gammon steaks, 2 portions, 200 g / 7 oz each	5	5	separate after 2½ minutes; cook covered with pierced cling film	2½–3
liver, 450 g / 1 lb	5	5	separate slices during defreezing	4
kidneys, 2–3	5	5	separate during defreezing; slice before cooking	3–5

JOINTS				
Defreezing and cooking guide per 450 g / 1 lb				
meat	defrost minutes	standing minutes	cooking in minutes on full	standing minutes
beef	9	10	rare: 4–5 medium: 7 well done: 9	10
lamb	10	5	7–9	10
pork	8–9	5	7–9	10
gammon	8–10	10	7	10
chicken	7–8	10, then wash thoroughly	6–7	5
turkey	thaw naturally	wash thoroughly	6–7	5

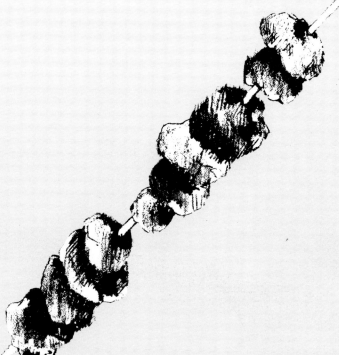

FISH/DEFREEZING AND COOKING GUIDE

The delicate flesh of fish and seafood requires only the minimum of cooking. Microwaving fish ensures that it retains all its succulence and flavour. Whole fish and fish steaks can be brushed with melted butter with a little lemon juice and herbs added, or poached in cream or wine for a richer taste. The fish is cooked when the flesh parts easily at the prod of a wooden cocktail stick. The centre will still be translucent – cooking will be completed after 5 – 10 minutes standing time.

Always arrange fish in a dish with the thinnest parts to the centre and cover with cling film. Pierce in 2 or 3 places to allow the steam to escape. Turn the dish or rearrange the fish half way through cooking time. When cooking whole fish, make 2 or 3 long diagonal slits in the skin to prevent it from bursting and shield the head and tail with foil.

Take care not to overcook fish otherwise it will become dry and tough. Avoid cooking fish in batter as it does not crisp, and remember that you can't deep fry in a microwave. Salmon and halibut juices run out of the fish during cooking (whether in a microwave or by a conventional method). To stop the juices spoiling the appearance of the fish, line the dish with kitchen paper and turn the fish over to serve.

FISH
Refreezing and cooking guide

fish	weight	defrost minutes	standing minutes	cooking in minutes on full
bass		5 – 6	15	5 – 6
bream		10, 5,	stand 20, stand 30	10 – 12
cod fillets		4 – 5	5	4 – 6
cod steaks		5	5	6
crab claws		5	5	2 – 3
crab, dressed	100 g / 4 oz	2	10	—
haddock fillets		4 – 5	5	5 – 7
haddock steaks		4 – 5	5	4 – 7
halibut steaks		4 – 5	5	4 – 5
hake steaks		4 – 5	5	4 – 6
kipper	1	—	—	1 – 2
kipper fillets (boil-in-the-bag)	200 g / 7 oz	3	5	3
mackerel		6 – 8	8 – 10	4 – 5
mullet		6 – 8	8 – 10	4 – 6
mussels		5	5	—
plaice fillets		4 – 5	5	4
prawns		5	5	—
salmon steaks		5	5	4 – 5
salmon trout	1 kg / 2 lb	8 – 10, 5,	stand 20, stand 30	7 – 10
scampi		5	5	2 – 3
scallops		5	5	5 – 7
snapper		6 – 8	8 – 10	5 – 7
sole		5 – 6	8 – 10	4
trout		6 – 8	8 – 10	7

PASTA, RICE AND PULSES/ COOKING GUIDE

Pasta, rice and pulses take the same time to cook in a microwave oven as they do by conventional methods, but with pasta and rice, especially, there are distinct advantages in using your new appliance. You avoid a kitchen full of steam and sticky saucepans. If you follow the instructions you should end up with perfectly cooked fluffy rice and tasty *al dente* pasta – particularly pleasing to cooks who find their rice always sticks together in a soggy lump and their pasta is either slimy or hard – or both! Test the food during standing time, and when it is cooked to your taste, drain off any remaining water. A sauce can then be added and the rice or pasta served up in its cooking dish.

Always use a large deep bowl and cover with either a lid or cling film slit in 2 or 3 places to allow the steam to escape. Leftovers can be reheated without adding extra water and without danger of them becoming hard and dried out – this is another advantage over using conventional cooking methods. Frozen rice and pasta can be reheated in the same way. If you are using fresh – as opposed to dried – pasta, halve the cooking times given in the chart.

COOKING GUIDE PER 225 G/8 OZ

food	boiling salted water to add	cooking in minutes on full	standing minutes
long grain rice	725 ml / 1¼ pint	14	5
brown rice	900 ml / 1½ pint	30	5
American rice	600 ml / 1 pint	12	5
egg noodles & tagliatelle	600 ml / 1 pint with 2 tsp oil	6–8	2–3
spaghetti	1 litre / 1¾ pint with 2 tsp oil	12	5–10
pasta shells and shapes	1 litre / 1¾ pint with 2 tsp oil	12–14	5–10
macaroni	1 litre / 1¾ pint with 2 tsp oil	12–15	2–3
lasagne	1 litre / 1¾ pint with 2 tsp oil	9	2

BREAD AND CAKES

Bread, cakes and biscuits can be cooked successfully in the microwave, but they will not brown. Colouring such as treacle or brown sugar can be added to cake mixtures and cakes can be decorated to make them look more attractive. Bread can be sprinkled with poppy or sesame seeds or finished off under the grill.

Bread can be made in half the time it takes with conventional methods. Proving can be speeded up by giving the dough 15-second bursts in the oven and allowing it to rest for 10 – 15 minutes in between. If you prefer, you can prove your bread in the microwave and then bake it in your conventional oven – but remember not to use a baking pan in the microwave. To thaw a loaf of bread, wrap it in cling film (plastic wrap) and place in the oven on defrost for 4 minutes, turning every minute. Allow to stand for 8 minutes.

The texture of cakes cooked in the microwave is light and airy and fruit cakes are rich and moist. Mixtures with a softer dropping consistency are more successful. Beware of overcooking – the surface of the cake will be moist when you remove it from the oven, but this will dry out during standing time due to residual heat. Test with a fine skewer after you have allowed the cake to stand – if it comes out clean, the cake is ready. Choose a large dish that will not be more than half filled by the mixture – a soufflé dish is ideal – and grease it well or line it with cling film or greased waxed paper.

Pastry is more trouble than it is worth to cook in the microwave, and it is recommended that flan cases be baked first in the conventional manner.

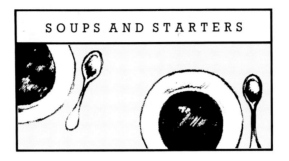

SOUPS AND STARTERS

VICHYSSOISE

Serves 4 / Set: full
3 cups / 350 g / 12 oz potatoes, peeled and diced
1 onion, sliced
½ cucumber, peeled and diced
3 leeks, trimmed, washed and sliced
4 tbs / 50 g / 2 oz butter
4 tbs water
4¼ cups / 1 litre / 1¾ pint chicken stock
salt / freshly ground black pepper
⅝ cup / 150 ml / ¼ pint single cream
2 tbs chives, chopped

1 Place the potatoes in a bowl with the onion, cucumber, leeks, butter and water. Cover and cook for 8 – 10 minutes, stirring once.

2 Add the stock and season. Cover and cook for 5 minutes, then blend in a liquidiser. Adjust seasoning and chill well.

3 Serve cold with a swirl of cream and sprinkled with chives.

TOMATO, CARROT AND ORANGE SOUP

Serves 4 / Set: full
2 425 g / 15 oz cans tomatoes, mashed with juice
2 cups / 225 g / 8 oz carrots, chopped
juice of 1 orange
bayleaf
salt / freshly ground black pepper
2½ cups / 600 ml / 1 pint chicken stock
rind of half an orange, finely grated
single (cereal) cream

1 Place tomatoes, carrots, orange juice, bayleaf and seasoning in a bowl. Cover with cling film (plastic wrap) slit in 2 or 3 places and cook for 15 minutes, or until carrots are soft, stirring once.

2 Remove the bayleaf and blend the mixture in a liquidiser. Return to the bowl with the stock and orange rind. Check seasoning. Cook for 4 minutes and serve hot or cold with a swirl of cream.

SIMPLE LENTIL SOUP

Serves 4 / Set: full
1½ cups / 225 g / 8 oz brown lentils, soaked overnight
6¼ cups / 1.5 l / 2½ pints water
2 chicken bouillon cubes
2 tbs / 25 g / 1 oz butter
squeeze of lemon juice
2 onions, sliced
2 cloves garlic, chopped
salt / freshly ground black pepper
fresh parsley, roughly chopped

1 Drain and rinse lentils. Place in a large bowl with water and bouillon cubes. Cook for 20 minutes, topping up water if necessary, or until lentils are mushy.

2 Place butter in a bowl and cook for 1 minute. Add lemon juice and stir in onion and garlic. Cook for 3 minutes.

3 Stir onion and garlic into lentils and season. Cook, covered, for 3 – 5 minutes. Serve with a generous garnish of chopped parsley.

TUSCAN VEGETABLE SOUP

Serves 4 – 6 / Set: full
2 tbs / 25 g / 1 oz butter
1½ cups / 100 g / 4 oz cabbage, roughly shredded
15 oz / 425 g can of butter (canneletti) beans, drained
1 cup / 100 g / 4 oz potatoes, diced
1 cup / 100 g / 4 oz carrots, scraped and sliced
½ cup / 100 g / 4 oz onions, sliced
1 – 2 cloves garlic, chopped
425 g / 15 oz can tomatoes, drained and mashed
salt / freshly ground black pepper
2½ - 3¾ cups / 600 – 900 ml / 1 – 1½ pint hot beef stock
1 slice crusty bread per serving

1 Place butter and vegetables in a large bowl. Cover and cook for 10 minutes, stirring once.

2 Season and add stock. Cover and cook for 25 minutes, or until carrots are soft, stirring once. Check seasoning.

3 Arrange bread slices in soup bowls. Pour over soup. Serve and offer parmesan cheese.

CORIANDER MUSHROOMS

Serves 4 / Set: full
1 tbs butter or ghee
1 tbs coriander seeds
⅝ cup / 150 ml / ¼ pint water
2 tbs olive oil
juice of 1 lemon
6 black peppercorns
1 small onion, finely chopped
1 clove garlic, finely chopped
6 cups / 450 g / 1 lb button mushrooms, wiped
chopped fresh coriander or parsley

1 On a conventional hob, melt the butter or ghee in a frying pan. When hot, stir in the coriander seeds and fry, stirring for 1 – 2 minutes.

2 Stir all the ingredients except for the mushrooms and fresh coriander into a bowl. Cook in the oven for 5 minutes. Stir in the mushrooms. Cook for 4 minutes.

3 Allow to stand until cool. Garnish with fresh coriander and serve with triangles of hot toast.

CORN ON THE COB WITH HERB BUTTER

Serves 4 / Set: full
½ cup / 100 g / 4 oz butter
4 corn on the cob, fresh or frozen
3 tbs finely chopped mixed fresh herbs

1 Cut up the butter and place in a small dish. Cook for 1 minute.

2 Brush the corn with some of the melted butter and wrap individually in waxed paper. Pack into a shallow dish. Cover and cook, for 10 minutes if fresh or 12 if frozen, until grains are tender when pierced.

3 Transfer corn to serving dishes.

4 Stir herbs into remaining butter and cook for 30 seconds. Pour herb butter over corn to serve.

CHICKEN LIVER PATE

Serves 4 / Set: full
225 g / ½ lb chicken livers
1 small onion, chopped
2 cloves garlic, chopped
⅝ cup / 150 g / 5 oz butter
2 tsp fresh thyme, chopped
salt / freshly ground black pepper
1 tbs port
1 tbs cream
sprigs of fresh thyme
juniper berries

1 Place the livers, onion, garlic, half the butter and the thyme in a bowl. Cover and cook for 5 minutes, stirring once.

2 Place mixture in a liquidiser with seasoning, port and cream and blend until smooth. Divide between 4 individual dishes.

3 Place remaining butter in a bowl and cook for 30 seconds until melted. Pour over the pâté and chill. Garnish with fresh thyme and juniper berries and serve with crusty French bread.

KIPPER PATE

Serves 4 / Set: medium
4 frozen kipper fillets
1 onion, finely chopped
2 tbs / 25 g / 1 oz butter
1 tbs lemon juice
½ cup / 75 g / 3 oz full fat cream cheese
1 tbs sherry
salt / freshly ground black pepper
parsley

1 Place the kippers, onion, butter and lemon juice in a dish, cover and cook on medium for 8 – 10 minutes, turning once.

2 Purée the kippers and onions with the cream cheese and sherry in a blender and season to taste.

3 Fill 4 individual dishes with the pâté and garnish with sprigs of parsley. Chill and serve with hot toast.

MOULES A LA MARINIERE

Serves 2 / Set: full

5 cups / 1.25 l / 2 pints mussels
4 tbs / 50 g / 2 oz butter
1 onion, chopped
1 clove garlic, chopped
a handful of fresh parsley, chopped
freshly ground black pepper
1 glass dry white wine

1 Clean mussels thoroughly under cold running water, scraping away beards. Discard mussels that are open or broken.

2 Place the butter in a large bowl and cook for 1 minute. Add the onion, garlic, parsley, pepper and wine. Cover and cook for 2 minutes. Add mussels, cover and cook for about 3 minutes until shells are open, giving the dish a good stir halfway through.

3 Serve with French bread to mop up the soup and provide a dish for the discarded shells.

INDIVIDUAL CRAB SOUFFLES

Serves 3 – 6 / Set: full
2 tbs / 25 g / 1 oz butter
4 tbs / 25 g / 1 oz flour
salt / freshly ground black pepper
¼ cup / 75 ml / ⅛ pint milk
2 egg yolks
½ cup / 100 g / 4 oz can crabmeat, flaked
1 cup / 25 g / 4 oz Gruyère cheese, grated
3 egg whites
paprika

1 Butter 6 individual dishes. Place the butter in a large bowl and cook for 1 minute. Stir in the flour and season. Cook for 1 – 2 minutes.

2 Carefully blend in the milk. Cook for 2 – 3 minutes, stirring, until the sauce thickens.

3 Stir the egg yolks, crab and cheese into the sauce. Allow to cool.

4 Whisk the egg whites until stiff and fold them in to the mixture. Divide between the dishes, dust with paprika and cook on medium for 7 – 9 minutes until done. Serve at once.

PRAWNS OR SHRIMPS IN WHISKY

Serves 4 / Set: full
4 tbs / 50 g / 2 oz butter
1 small onion, chopped
2¼ cups / 350 g / 12 oz prawns or shrimps, shelled
4 tbs whipping cream
4 tbs whisky

1 Place butter in a dish and cook for 1 minute. Add onion and cook for 3 minutes.

2 Stir in the prawns or shrimps and cook for 2 – 3 minutes, until hot. Divide between 4 small preheated dishes.

3 Mix cream and whisky together in a small dish and cook for 30 seconds. Pour over prawns or shrimps and serve hot.

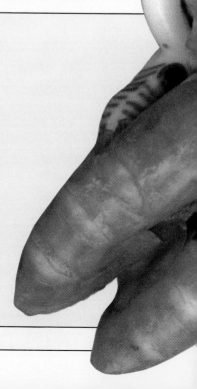

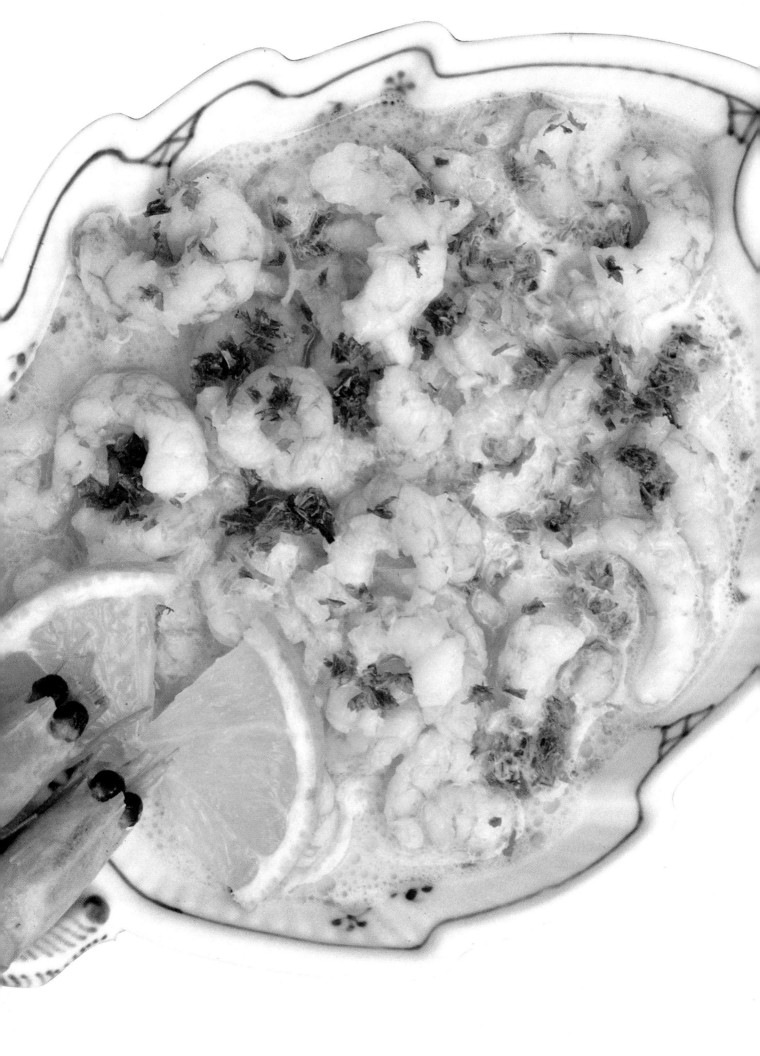

FISH

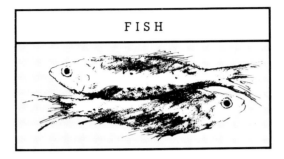

Spicy cod *30*

Portuguese fish casserole with rice *31*

Squid provencal *32*

Soused herring *33*

Trout with almonds *34*

Fillets of sole in mustard cream sauce *36*

Tuna, corn and pepper flan *38*

Suffolk fish pie *39*

Paella *40*

Mackerel with orange *42*

Cod with courgettes *43*

SPICY COD

Serves 4 / Set: full
4 cod steaks
1 onion, sliced
1 clove garlic, chopped
small can of tomatoes, mashed up with juice
1 tbs tomato paste
salt / freshly ground black pepper
1 tsp turmeric
1 tsp garam masala
fresh coriander or parsley

1 Place onion, garlic, tomatoes and tomato paste in a large shallow dish and season with salt and pepper. Cover and cook for 5 minutes, stirring once.

2 Rub cod steaks with turmeric and garam masala. Place in the dish and cover with the vegetables. Cook, covered, for 5 minutes or until fish is done.

3 Garnish with fresh coriander or parsley and serve.

PORTUGUESE FISH CASSEROLE WITH RICE

Serves / 4 Set: full and medium high
900 g / 2 lb cod fillets, skinned and cut into chunks
5 tbs olive oil
1 tbs cider vinegar
salt / freshly ground black pepper
1 large onion, sliced
1 large green pepper, cut into bite-size pieces
1 large red pepper, cut into bite-size pieces
2 – 3 cloves garlic, chopped
¾ cup / 175 g / 6 oz long-grain rice
1⅞ cup / 450 ml / ¾ pint boiling fish stock or water
425 g / 15 oz can tomatoes, mashed
tomato wedges, optional
chopped parsley, optional

1 Mix together 3 tbs of the oil with the vinegar and seasoning. Put the fish and half the onion, peppers and garlic in a large bowl and pour over the dressing. Leave to marinate for half an hour.

2 Place the rest of the oil, onion, garlic and peppers in a bowl. Cover and cook on full power for 3 – 4 minutes until onion is transparent. Add rice and fish stock or water, stir and cook for 7 minutes.

3 Drain the rice and reserve the cooking liquor. Mix rice with fish and vegetables in a casserole. Add tomatoes and enough tomato juice and reserved stock or water to just cover. Check seasoning.

4 Cover the casserole and cook on medium high for 15 minutes or until rice is tender. Allow to stand for 10 minutes before serving.

5 Garnish with tomato wedges and chopped parsley.

Portuguese Fish casserole

SQUID PROVENÇAL

Serves 4 / Set: full
1 tbs olive oil
1 onion, chopped
2 cloves garlic, chopped
425 g / 15 oz can tomatoes, drained and mashed
1 tbs tomato paste
2 – 3 tbs dry white wine
freshly ground black pepper
2 tbs parsley, chopped
4 squid, cleaned and sliced
boiled rice

1 Pour oil into a dish and stir in onion and garlic. Cook for 3 minutes.

2 Stir in tomatoes, tomato paste, wine, pepper and parsley. Cook for 3 minutes.

3 Add squid and cook for 4 minutes, stirring once. Allow to stand for 5 minutes before serving on a bed of boiled rice.

Soused Herring

SOUSED HERRING

Serves 4 / Set: full
4 herrings, filleted
salt / freshly ground black pepper
⅝ cup / 150 ml / ¼ pint cider vinegar
⅝ cup / 150 ml / ¼ pint water
½ tsp pickling spice
1 bayleaf
1 large cooking apple, peeled and sliced
1 onion, sliced

1 Roll up the fillets and secure with cocktail sticks or toothpicks.

2 Season the fish and place in a shallow dish with the vinegar, water, pickling spice and bayleaf. Top with apple and onion.

3 Cover with cling film (plastic wrap) and slit in 2 or 3 places. Cook for 8 minutes, turning once. Allow to cool.

4 Chill and drain before serving with salad and hot new potatoes.

TROUT WITH ALMONDS

Serves 4 / Set: full
4 tbs / 50 g / 2 oz butter
1/3 cup / 50 g / 2 oz flaked almonds
juice of half a lemon
4 trout, cleaned, but with the heads left on
salt / freshly ground black pepper

1 Place the butter in a large oblong dish. Cook for 1 minute. Stir in almonds and cook for 1 minute.

2 Stir in lemon juice. Add trout, baste and season. Cover with cling film (plastic wrap) and slit in 2 or 3 places. Cook for 2 – 3 minutes.

3 Turn fish over, baste and return dish to oven, giving it half a turn. Cook for a further 2 – 3 minutes, depending on the size of the fish. Spoon almonds and butter over fish and serve.

FILLETS OF SOLE IN MUSTARD CREAM SAUCE

Serves 4 / Set: full
4 sole, filleted
1 small onion, chopped
1 small carrot, chopped
bayleaf
1 small glass dry white wine
⅝ cup / 150 ml / ¼ pint water
salt / freshly ground black pepper
2 tbs / 25 g / 1 oz butter
2 tbs flour
3 tbs single (cereal) cream
2 tsp English mustard

1 Roll up the fillets and place in a shallow dish with onion, carrot, bayleaf, wine, water and seasoning. Cover and cook for 5 minutes. Drain and reserve liquid, discarding vegetables and bayleaf.

2 Place butter in a bowl and cook for 1 minute. Stir in flour. Gradually add fish liquor. Cook for 3 minutes until thickened, stirring every minute.

3 Stir in cream and mustard and pour over fish. Cook for 1 minute before serving.

TUNA, CORN AND PEPPER FLAN

Serves 6 / Set: full
18 cm / 7 in pastry crust (pie shell), cooked
2 tbs / 25 g / 1 oz butter
4 tbs / 25 g / 1 oz flour
⅝ cup / 150 ml / ¼ pint milk
small can corn and peppers, drained
175 g / 7 oz can tuna, drained and flaked
2 large eggs, beaten
salt / freshly ground black pepper
1 cup / 100 g / 4 oz Edam cheese, grated
thin tomato slices

1 Place butter in a large bowl and cook on full for 1 minute. Blend in flour, then gradually stir in milk. Cover and cook on full for 3 minutes.

2 Add corn and peppers and tuna. Stir in eggs, seasoning and cheese.

3 Pour into pastry case and cook on medium for 5 minutes. Leave to stand for 5 minutes. Cook on full for a further 8 minutes or until filling has nearly set. Garnish with tomato slices. Allow to stand for 5 minutes before serving.

SUFFOLK FISH PIE

Serves 4 – 6 / Set: full

450 g / 1 lb smoked cod or haddock fillets, skinned
1¼ cup / 6 oz cooked prawns or shrimps, shelled
3 medium leeks, sliced
3 tbs water
6 cups / 750 g / 1½ lb potatoes, peeled and cubed

Sauce

5 tbs milk
2 tbs / 25 g / 1 oz butter
4 tbs / 25 g / 1 oz flour
salt / freshly ground black pepper
½ cup / 50 g / 2 oz Edam cheese, grated
parmesan cheese
milk

1 Place fish, prawns or shrimps and leeks in a large bowl. Cover and cook for 6 minutes, rearranging once. Flake fish and reserve the stock.

2 Place water, salt and potatoes in a large bowl. Cover and cook for 10 minutes. Set aside, covered.

3 To make the sauce, use fish stock to make up to 1¼ cup / 300 ml / ½ pint with milk.

4 Place butter in a bowl and cook for 30 seconds. Stir in flour, fish liquor and seasoning. Cook for 3 minutes, stirring twice.

5 Combine fish, vegetables, sauce and grated cheese in a deep pie dish (plate). Stir well.

6 Mash potatoes with butter, milk and seasoning to taste. Spread potatoes over fish mixture, sprinkle with parmesan cheese and cook, uncovered, for 4 minutes. Brown under the grill (broiler) before serving.

PAELLA

Serves 6 / Set: full
1 large onion, chopped
3 cloves garlic, chopped
1 tbs olive oil
1 cup / 225 g / 8 oz long-grain rice
a few strands of saffron or 1 tsp turmeric
3⅛ cups / 750 ml / 1¼ pint hot chicken stock
salt / freshly ground black pepper
⅔ cup / 100 g / 4 oz frozen peas
1¼ cup / 150 g / 6 oz cooked prawns or shrimps, shelled
1½ cups / 175 g / 6 oz cooked mussels
1½ cups / 175 g / 6 oz cooked clams
⅔ cup / 100 g / 4 oz cooked chicken, cut into bite-sized pieces
lemon wedges

1 Place onion and garlic in a large bowl, pour over oil, stir, cover and cook for 3 minutes.

2 Stir in rice, saffron or turmeric, stock and seasoning. Cover and cook for 10 minutes, stirring twice. Set aside.

3 Place peas in a bowl, cover and cook for 3 minutes. Reserving some seafood in shells to garnish, stir in prawns or shrimps, mussels, clams and chicken, cover and cook for 6 minutes.

4 Drain. Stir into rice and garnish with remaining seafood and lemon wedges.

MACKEREL WITH ORANGES

Serves 4 / Set: full
4 mackerel, cleaned
⅝ cup / 150 ml / ¼ pint oil
⅝ cup / 150 ml / ¼ pint orange juice
grated rind of 1 orange
a few drops of Tabasco sauce
salt / freshly ground black pepper
½ cup / 50 g / 2 oz black olives
thin orange slices

1 Make slanting incisions with a sharp knife across both sides of each fish. Place in a large shallow dish.

2 Mix together the oil, orange juice, rind and Tabasco and season with salt and pepper. Pour the marinade over the fish and marinate for 2 hours, turning occasionally.

3 Baste the fish and cover with cling film (plastic wrap) slit in 2 or 3 places. Cook for 2 – 3 minutes.

4 Turn fish over, baste and return to oven, giving dish a half turn. Cool for a further 2 – 3 minutes, depending on the size of the fish. Spoon marinade over fish and serve garnished with olives and orange slices.

COD WITH COURGETTES (ZUCCHINI)

Serves 4 / Set: full
4 cod cutlets
juice of 1 lemon
6 tbs / 75 g / 3 oz butter
1 onion, thinly sliced
4 courgettes (zucchini), cut into matchsticks, drained and chopped
1 can anchovy fillets
1 tbs capers
freshly ground black pepper
lemon slices

1 Place cod in a large shallow dish and sprinkle with lemon juice. Cover with cling film (plastic wrap) slit in 2 or 3 places. Cook for 3 minutes. Turn fish over and set aside.

2 Place butter in a dish and cook for 1 minute. Add onion and courgettes (zucchini) and cook for 3 minutes. Stir in anchovies and capers and season with pepper. Pour over fish.

3 Return cod to oven, altering position of dish. Cook for 3 minutes, depending on the size of the fish. Garnish with lemon slices and serve with mashed potato.

CHEESE AND EGGS

CHEESE FONDUE

Serves 4 / Set: full
1 clove garlic, finely chopped
⅝ cup / 150 ml / ¼ pint dry white wine
2 cups / 225 g / 8 oz Gruyère cheese, grated
2 tsp cornflour (cornstarch)
2 tbs brandy
freshly ground black pepper
nutmeg

1 Place garlic and wine in a bowl and cook for 2 minutes.

2 Add cheese. Cook for 4 minutes, stirring 3 times, until cheese has melted.

3 Mix together cornflour (cornstarch), brandy, pepper and nutmeg. Stir into cheese. Cook for 4 minutes.

4 Serve with French bread cut into bite-sized pieces and accompany with a crisp salad. Provide each guest with a fondue fork or kebab stick for spearing the bread.

SOUFFLE OMELETTE FINES HERBES

Serves 1 – 2 / Set: full

4 eggs, separated

1 – 2 tbs milk

salt / freshly ground black pepper

2 tbs mixed fresh herbs, chopped

1 tbs / 15 g / ½ oz butter

fresh herbs to garnish

1 Mix egg yolks with milk, seasoning and herbs.

2 Place butter in a 20 cm/8 in shallow dish and cook for 1 minute. Brush butter round sides and base of dish.

3 Beat egg whites until stiff and fold into yolk mixture. Pour into dish, cover with cling film (plastic wrap) and slit in 2 or 3 places. Cook for 2 minutes.

4 Using a fork, draw the edges of the egg to the middle. Cover and cook for a further 1 minute or until barely cooked.

5 Serve garnished with fresh herbs.

SCRAMBLED EGGS WITH ANCHOVIES

Serves 4 / Set: full
8 eggs
2 tbs milk
½ tsp garam masala
freshly ground black pepper
can of anchovies, drained and chopped
2 tbs / 25 g / 1 oz butter

1 Whisk eggs. Beat in milk and season with garam masala and pepper. Stir in anchovies.

2 Place butter in a shallow oval dish and cook for 1 minute. Stir in egg mixture and cook for about 3 minutes, or until nearly cooked, stirring every minute.

3 Allow to stand for 1 minute before serving with triangles of hot toast.

Scrambled Egg with Anchovies

LEEK AND STILTON QUICHE

Serves 6 / Set: full and medium
18 cm / 7 in pastry crust (pie shell), cooked
4 tbs / 50 g / 2 oz butter
3 leeks, trimmed, washed and sliced
4 tbs / 25 g / 1 oz flour
⅝ cup / 300 ml / ½ pint milk
⅝ cup / 50 g / 2 oz stilton, crumbled
2 eggs, beaten
salt / freshly ground black pepper
parsley
sliced tomatoes

1 Place half the butter in a bowl and cook for 1 minute. Stir in leeks and cook for 3 – 4 minutes, stirring once, until cooked. Remove leeks and set aside.

2 Place remaining butter in a bowl and cook for 1 minute. Stir in flour and gradually add milk. Stir in cheese, eggs and leeks and season well.

3 Pour filling into pastry case and cook on medium for 5 minutes. Allow to stand for 5 minutes. Cook for a further 8 minutes, or until filling has nearly set. Allow to stand for 5 minutes before serving, garnished with parsley and sliced tomatoes.

POACHED EGGS ON SPINACH WITH HOLLANDAISE SAUCE

Serves 4 / Set: full
½ cup / 225 g / 8 oz frozen spinach, thawed and drained
salt / freshly ground black pepper
4 eggs
Hollandaise sauce
2 egg yolks
juice of half a lemon
½ cup / 100 g / 4 oz butter, cut into small pieces
pinch of nutmeg

1 Divide spinach between 4 individual dishes and cook for 1½ minutes. Season with salt and pepper.

2 Break the eggs onto the spinach and prick the yolks. Cover the individual dishes with cling film (plastic wrap).

3 To make the sauce, place the egg yolks in a basin with the lemon juice. Prick the yolks and cook for 30 seconds. Beat until smooth.

4 Arrange the individual dishes in the middle of the oven and cook for 2 minutes.

5 Meanwhile, beat the butter into the sauce piece by piece. Beat in the nutmeg. Spoon the sauce over the eggs and serve.

PIPERADE

Serves 2 – 4 / Set: full
1 green pepper
1 red pepper
2 tbs olive oil
1 Spanish onion, finely sliced
2 cloves garlic, chopped
4 large tomatoes, peeled and sliced
5 eggs
2 – 4 tsp fresh basil, chopped
salt / freshly ground black pepper
fresh basil leaves

1 Remove pith and seeds from peppers and slice finely.

2 Pour olive oil into a shallow oval dish and cook for 1 minute. Stir in onion, garlic and peppers and cook for 2 minutes. Stir in tomatoes and cook for a further 2 minutes, or until vegetables are cooked.

3 Beat eggs with basil and season. Stir egg mixture into vegetables. Cook for about 3 minutes or until nearly cooked, stirring every minute. Allow to stand for 1 minute, garnish with fresh basil and serve with a crisp green salad.

CAULIFLOWER CHEESE SOUFFLE

Serves 4 – 6 / Set: various
1 small cauliflower
2 - 3 tbs water
6 tbs / 40 g / 1½ oz flour
salt
1⅞ cup / 450 ml / ¾ pint milk
¾ cup / 75 g / 3 oz strong Cheddar cheese, grated
5 eggs, separated
1 tbs brown breadcrumbs

1 Discard leaves and stalk of cauliflower and break into florets. Place in a bowl with 2 – 3 tbs water and cook, covered, on medium high for 10 minutes, stirring once. Drain, and reserve cauliflower.

2 Place flour and salt in a bowl. Stir in the milk and cook on full, stirring every 2 minutes, for about 5 minutes, or until thickened.

3 Stir in the cheese, reserving 1 tbs for the topping, and the cauliflower and cook on full for 1 minute, or until cheese has melted.

4 Beat egg yolks and beat into cauliflower cheese mixture. Whisk egg whites until stiff. Fold gently into mixture.

5 Pour the mixture into a large soufflé dish. Sprinkle with remaining grated cheese and brown breadcrumbs. Cook on low for 10 minutes, then on medium for 5 – 10 minutes, giving dish a quarter turn every 5 minutes. The soufflé should appear set but not hard. Serve at once with a salad.

WELSH RAREBIT

Serves 4 / Set: full and medium
4 slices wholewheat toast
4 slices ham
2 cups / 225 g / 8 oz Cheddar cheese, grated
1 tbs / 15 g / ½ oz butter
salt / freshly ground black pepper
½ tsp Worcestershire sauce
½ tsp paprika
3 tbs single (cereal) cream
tomato wedges
sprigs of watercress

1 Top each slice of toast with a slice of ham and keep warm.

2 Place the cheese and butter in a bowl and cook on full, stirring every minute, for 3 minutes until cheese has melted.

3 Stir in seasoning and cream and cook on medium for 8 minutes, stirring every minute, until smooth and creamy.

4 Top the toast and ham with the cheese mixture and serve garnished with tomato wedges and sprigs of watercress.

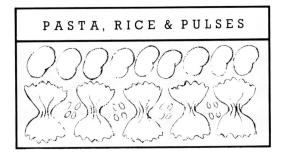

PASTA, RICE & PULSES

Spaghetti bolognese *58*

Macaroni cheese with tuna fish *59*

Tagliatelli with gorgonzola *60*

Chicken lasagne *62*

Pasta shells with ham and mushrooms *63*

Kedgeree *64*

Risotto *66*

Cabbage parcels *68*

Aduki bean casserole with peas *69*

SPAGHETTI BOLOGNESE

Serves 4 / Set: full
2 tbs oil
1 onion, chopped
2 cloves garlic, chopped
1 stick celery, chopped
1 carrot, chopped
½ green pepper, chopped
2 cups / 100 g / 4 oz mushrooms, chopped
4 strips streaky bacon, diced
450 g / 1 lb minced (ground) beef
425 g / 15 oz can tomatoes
1 tbs tomato paste
1 tsp dried mixed herbs
salt / freshly ground black pepper
1 tbs red wine
2½ cups / 275 g / 10 oz spaghetti
approx. 7 cups / 1.5 l / 2¾ pint boiling water
1 tbs / 15 g / ½ oz butter
parmesan cheese

1 Place the oil in a large bowl and heat for 1 minute.

2 Add onion, garlic, celery, carrot, pepper and mushrooms and cook for 3 minutes.

3 Add bacon, stir and cook for 3 minutes. Add beef, tomatoes (reserving some juice to add later if necessary), tomato paste, seasoning and red wine. Cook for 12 minutes. Blend the sauce in a liquidiser and adjust seasoning.

4 Place spaghetti in a deep bowl and pour over water. Cook, covered, for 8 – 10 minutes until just beginning to soften. Allow to stand, covered, for a further 8 – 10 minutes.

5 When pasta is almost ready, re-heat sauce for 2 minutes.

6 Drain spaghetti, toss in butter and season with freshly ground black pepper. Serve in warmed individual pasta bowls topped with a helping of bolognese sauce. Offer parmesan cheese to sprinkle on top.

MACARONI CHEESE WITH TUNA FISH

Serves 4 / Set: full
1 cup / 250 g / 8 oz macaroni
2½ cups / 600 ml / 1 pint boiling water
1 tbs oil
2 tbs / 25 g / 1 oz butter
4 tbs / 25 g / 1 oz flour
1¼ cups / 300 ml / ½ pint milk
¾ cup / 75 g / 3 oz Edam cheese, grated
1 can tuna, drained and flaked
salt / freshly ground black pepper

1 Place macaroni in a large shallow dish. Pour over water and add salt and oil. Cook, covered, for 10 minutes. Allow to stand for 3 minutes. Drain.

2 Meanwhile, place butter in a bowl and cook for 1 minute. Blend in flour and gradually stir in milk. Cook for 6 minutes, stirring every minute.

3 Stir in the cheese and tuna fish and season with pepper. Stir in the macaroni. Cook for 3 – 4 minutes, then brown under the grill (broiler) before serving.

TAGLIATELLI WITH GORGONZOLA

Serves 4 / Set: full
2 - 2½ cups / 350 g / 12 oz tagliatelli
boiling water to cover
1 tbs oil
2 cups / 250 g / 8 oz ripe gorgonzola cheese
⅝ cup / 150 ml / ¼ pint cream
salt / freshly ground black pepper
chopped parsley

1 Place tagliatelli in a deep bowl with the boiling water. Add salt and oil and cook, covered, for 12 – 15 minutes, until barely cooked. Allow to stand for 10 – 15 minutes, covered. Drain.

2 Meanwhile, crumble up cheese and blend in a liquidiser with the cream. Toss the pasta in the sauce and cook for 1 – 2 minutes until hot.

3 Add chopped parsley, season with pepper and serve.

CHICKEN LASAGNE

Serves 4 / Set: full
350 g / 12 oz chicken
10 - 12 sheets / 175 g / 6 oz lasagne
3¼ cups / 900 ml / 1½ pint boiling water
2 tsp oil
3 tbs / 40 g / 1½ oz butter
1 onion, chopped
1 clove garlic, chopped
2 cups / 100 g / 4 oz mushrooms, sliced
1 tsp dried basil
6 tbs / 40 g / 1½ oz flour
1⅞ cups / 450 ml / ¾ pint milk
1 chicken stock (bouillon) cube
salt / freshly ground black pepper
¾ cup / 40 g / 1½ oz Edam cheese, grated
sprigs of fresh basil

1 Place chicken in a shallow dish. Cover and cook for 7 minutes, turning once. Allow to stand, covered, for 4 minutes. Remove skin and bones and chop meat.

2 Place the lasagne in a large oblong dish. Cover completely with water and add salt and oil. Cover and cook for 10 minutes. Allow to stand, covered, for 15 minutes. Drain and lay out on a clean tea towel.

3 Place butter in a bowl and cook for 1 minute. Stir in onion, garlic, mushrooms and thyme and cook for 2 minutes.

4 Stir in the flour and gradually add the milk, stirring. Crumble in the chicken stock (bouillon) cube. Cook for 4 minutes.

5 Stir in the chicken and season with pepper. Cook for 3 minutes.

6 Layer the lasagne and chicken sauce in the casserole dish, starting with a layer of lasagne and ending with a layer of sauce. Top with grated cheese. Cook for 1 – 2 minutes.

7 Brown the lasagne under the grill (broiler) and garnish with sprigs of fresh basil.

PASTA SHELLS WITH HAM AND MUSHROOMS

Serves 4 / Set: full and medium high
2½ cups / 350 g / 12 oz pasta shells
3¾ cups / 900 ml / 1½ pint boiling water
1 tbs oil
4 tbs / 50 g / 2 oz butter
1 small onion, chopped
1 stick celery, chopped
1⅓ cups / 75 g / 3 oz mushrooms, sliced
1 tbs / 25 g / 1 oz flour
1¼ cups / 300 ml / ½ pint milk
salt / freshly ground black pepper
1 - 1⅓ cups / 175 – 225 g / 6 – 8 oz ham, diced
⅓ cup / 50 g / 2 oz unsalted peanuts

1 Place pasta in a large bowl, pour over boiling water and add salt and oil. Cook for 8 – 10 minutes on medium high or until barely cooked. Drain, rinse with hot water and set aside.

2 Place half the butter in a large casserole and cook on full for 1 minute. Stir in onion, celery and mushrooms and cook on full for 3 minutes.

3 Place the remaining butter in a bowl and cook on full for 1 minute. Blend in flour and gradually stir in milk. Cook for 3 minutes on full, stirring every minute until thick and smooth. Season.

4 Add the pasta shells, ham and nuts to the vegetables. Stir. Mix in the sauce. Cook on medium high for 8 – 10 minutes. Allow to stand for 5 minutes before serving.

KEDGEREE

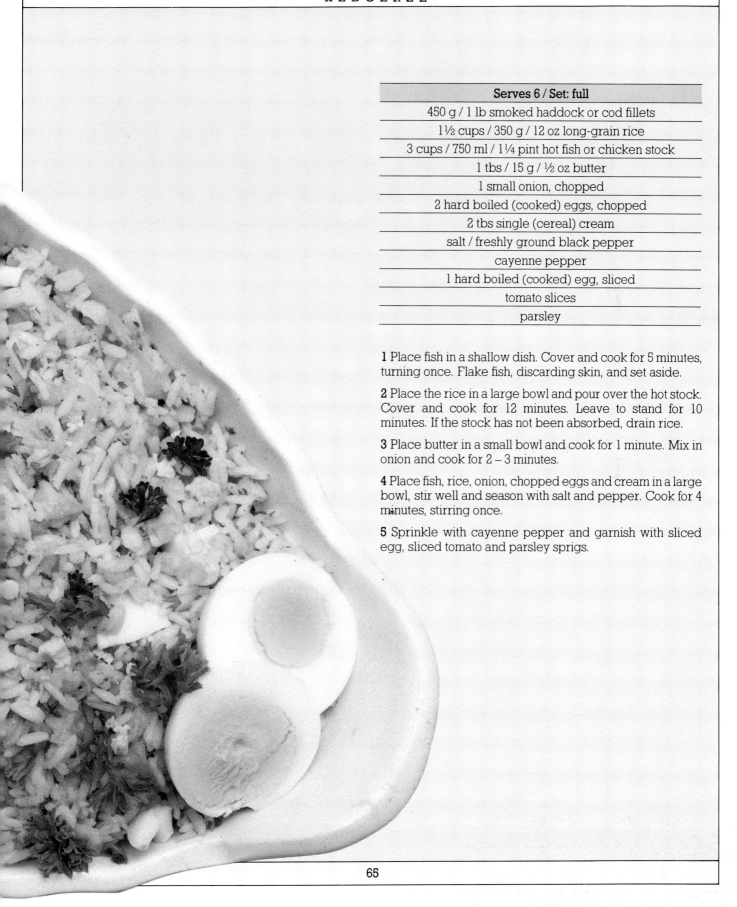

Serves 6 / Set: full
450 g / 1 lb smoked haddock or cod fillets
1½ cups / 350 g / 12 oz long-grain rice
3 cups / 750 ml / 1¼ pint hot fish or chicken stock
1 tbs / 15 g / ½ oz butter
1 small onion, chopped
2 hard boiled (cooked) eggs, chopped
2 tbs single (cereal) cream
salt / freshly ground black pepper
cayenne pepper
1 hard boiled (cooked) egg, sliced
tomato slices
parsley

1 Place fish in a shallow dish. Cover and cook for 5 minutes, turning once. Flake fish, discarding skin, and set aside.

2 Place the rice in a large bowl and pour over the hot stock. Cover and cook for 12 minutes. Leave to stand for 10 minutes. If the stock has not been absorbed, drain rice.

3 Place butter in a small bowl and cook for 1 minute. Mix in onion and cook for 2 – 3 minutes.

4 Place fish, rice, onion, chopped eggs and cream in a large bowl, stir well and season with salt and pepper. Cook for 4 minutes, stirring once.

5 Sprinkle with cayenne pepper and garnish with sliced egg, sliced tomato and parsley sprigs.

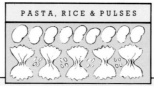

RISOTTO

Serves 4 / Set: full
4 tbs / 50 g / 2 oz butter
1 large onion, chopped
1 courgette (zucchini), diced
1 carrot, diced
1 large / 50 g / 2 oz tomato, peeled and chopped
1 cup / 50 g / 2 oz mushrooms, sliced
1¾ cups / 400 g / 14 oz long-grain rice
4⅜ cups / 750 ml / 1¾ pint hot chicken stock
1 tbs tomato paste
½ tsp oil
salt / freshly ground black pepper
1 tbs fresh herbs, chopped

1 Place the butter in a large bowl and cook for a minute. Stir in the vegetables, cover and cook for 8 minutes, stirring once.

2 Stir in the remaining ingredients, except the herbs. Cover and cook for 15 minutes, stirring once.

3 Allow to stand, covered, for 7 minutes. Fluff up the risotto with a fork and garnish with the herbs. Offer Worcestershire sauce.

CABBAGE PARCELS

Serves 4 / Set: full
1 young green cabbage
1 tbs / 15 g / ½ oz butter
1 onion, chopped
1 clove garlic, chopped
1⅓ cups / 75 g / 3 oz mushrooms, chopped
4 tbs flour
1¼ cups / 300 ml / ½ pint hot chicken stock
salt / freshly ground black pepper
¾ cup / 100 g / 4 oz cooked pork, chopped
1 cup / 175 g / 6 oz cooked rice

1 Remove the stalk and cook the cabbage in the conventional manner on the hob. Drain. Carefully detach the large leaves – the smaller ones can be used in a soup.

2 Place the butter, onion, garlic and mushrooms in a bowl and cook, covered, for 3 minutes. Stir in the flour and gradually add the stock, stirring. Season. Stir in the pork and rice and cook, uncovered, for 2 minutes.

3 Place a little mixture on each of the cabbage leaves. Fold the leaves over to make parcels and secure with thread.

4 Arrange parcels in a shallow dish, cover and cook for 7 minutes, giving the dish a half turn halfway through cooking time.

5 Allow to stand for 5 minutes. Carefully snip and remove the thread. Serve with tomato sauce (see page 82).

ADZUKI BEAN CASSEROLE WITH PEAS

Serves 4 / Set: full
⅔ cup / 150 g / 5 oz adzuki beans
½ cup / 75 g / 3 oz dried marrowfat peas
approx. 3 cups / 750 ml / 1¼ pint boiling water
chicken bouillon cube
salt / freshly ground black pepper
1 tbs oil
1 large onion, sliced
2 cloves garlic, sliced
2 cups / 100 g / 4 oz mushrooms, sliced
425 g / 15 oz can tomatoes, mashed and juice reserved
i tbs tomato paste
2 tsp fresh thyme
brown breadcrumbs
parmesan cheese

1 Soak adzuki beans and peas overnight, drain and rinse. Place in a casserole, pour over water, add bouillon cube and seasoning. Cook for 30 minutes, or until legumes are beginning to get mushy. Drain.

2 Place oil in a bowl and cook for 1 minute. Stir in onion, garlic and mushrooms and cook for 3 minutes. Stir in tomatoes, tomato paste and thyme and cook for 4 minutes.

3 Stir in beans and peas. Blend half the mixture in a liquidiser and return to the casserole. Mix well. If the consistency is too dry, add reserved tomato juice to moisten. Check seasoning.

4 Top with brown breadcrumbs and parmesan cheese and cook for 5 minutes. Serve with stir-fried shredded cabbage or Brussels sprouts and baked potatoes.

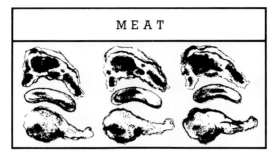

MEAT

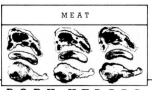

PORK KEBABS

Serves 4 / Set: full
3½ cups / 550 g / 1¼ lb leg of pork, cubed
juice of 2 lemons
3 tbs olive oil
salt / freshly ground black pepper
1 tsp dried oregano
1 small aubergine (egg plant), cut into bite-size pieces
1 small green pepper, cut into bite-size pieces
1 small red pepper, cut into bite-size pieces

1 Place the pork in a bowl with the lemon juice, oil, salt, pepper and oregano and marinate for 2 hours. Add the vegetables and toss in the marinade.

2 Thread the ingredients onto 6 wooden skewers and brush with the marinade. Place the kebabs in a shallow dish and cook for 11 minutes, turning and basting frequently. Serve with rice and a piquant green salad.

Serves 4 / Set: full
4 slices pork fillet
⅝ cup / 300 ml / ½ pint dry cider
juice of half a lemon
1 tbs mixed fresh herbs, chopped
3 tbs oil
1 carrot, sliced
1 onion, sliced
2 courgettes (zucchini), sliced
1 cooking apple, sliced
1 chicken bouillon cube
1 tsp cornflour (cornstarch)
salt / freshly ground black pepper

1 Marinate the pork in the cider, lemon juice and herbs for half an hour.

2 Pour oil into a large shallow casserole and cook for 1 minute. Stir in the vegetables and apple and cook for 3 minutes.

3 Add the pork and marinate and cook for 6 minutes, stirring once.

4 Crumble over the chicken bouillon cube, stir in cornflour and season well. Cover and cook for 15 minutes. Allow to stand for 5 minutes, rearrange the meat and cook for a further 5 minutes or until done. Serve with mashed potatoes.

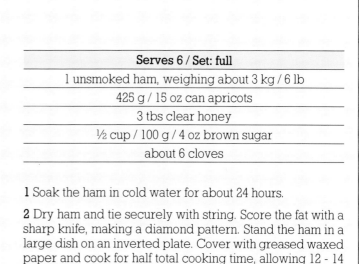

Serves 6 / Set: full
1 unsmoked ham, weighing about 3 kg / 6 lb
425 g / 15 oz can apricots
3 tbs clear honey
½ cup / 100 g / 4 oz brown sugar
about 6 cloves

1 Soak the ham in cold water for about 24 hours.

2 Dry ham and tie securely with string. Score the fat with a sharp knife, making a diamond pattern. Stand the ham in a large dish on an inverted plate. Cover with greased waxed paper and cook for half total cooking time, allowing 12 - 14 minutes per 450 g / 1 lb. Allow to stand for 30 minutes.

3 Drain apricots and reserve juice. Pour juice into a bowl with honey and cook for 3 minutes.

4 Brush the fat with the syrup, sprinkle with half sugar and insert the cloves into the score marks.

5 Return the ham to the dish, turning over to finish the cooking time.

6 Add the remaining sugar to the syrup and cook for 3 minutes, stirring once. Brush the fat with the glaze and leave to cool.

7 Decorate the ham with apricot halves, secured with wooden cocktail sticks or toothpicks, before serving.

SWEET AND SOUR SPARE RIBS

Serves 4 / Set: full
675 g / 1½ lb spare rib chops
2 tbs / 25 g / 1 oz butter
1 small onion, chopped
2 tbs / 25 g / 1 oz red or green pepper, chopped
2 tbs / 25 g / 1 oz carrot, chopped
4 cloves garlic, chopped
4 thin slices fresh ginger, chopped
3 tbs / 25 g / 1 oz cornflour (cornstarch)
1 tbs tomato ketchup
2 tbs / 25 g / 1 oz brown sugar
1 tbs sherry
3 tbs red wine vinegar
1 tbs soy sauce
salt

1 Place the ribs in a large shallow dish and cook for 5 minutes. Remove from the dish and cook for 1 minute. Stir in the butter, onion, pepper, carrot, garlic and ginger and cook for 3 minutes. Stir in the cornflour (cornstarch), then gradually stir in the other ingredients.

2 Add the chops to the sauce. Cook, covered, for 18 minutes, turning the chops and stirring the sauce once.

3 Serve with plain rice.

COQ AU VIN

Serves 4 / Set: full
8 chicken pieces
½ cup / 100 g / 4 oz salt pork or unsmoked bacon, rinded and cut into pieces
1 tbs flour
½ cup / 100 ml / 4 fl oz hot chicken stock
½ bottle red wine
small glass brandy
1 tsp tomato paste
2 bayleaves
1 tsp dried thyme
salt / freshly ground black pepper
2 cloves garlic, crushed
15 button onions
2⅔ cups / 175 g / 6 oz button mushrooms
fingers of toast

1 Place salt pork or bacon in a casserole and cook for 4 – 5 minutes until crisp. Remove, and blend flour with dripping until smooth.

2 Gradually stir in stock, wine and brandy. Stir in tomato paste, bayleaves, thyme, salt and pepper. Add garlic, onions and mushrooms. Cover and cook for 12 minutes.

3 Stir in crisp bacon and arrange chicken in the sauce. Cook, uncovered, for 12 minutes or until chicken is done.

4 Allow to stand for 10 minutes before serving, garnished with fingers of toast.

SAGE AND MOZZARELLA-STUFFED CHICKEN

Serves 4 / Set: full
1.5 – 2 kg / 3½ – 4 lb oven ready chicken
6 sage leaves
¼ - ½ cup / 25 - 50 g / 1 – 2 oz mozzarella cheese, sliced
2 tbs / 25 g / 1 oz butter
1 onion, chopped
1 cup / 50 g / 2 oz white breadcrumbs
2 tsp fresh sage, chopped
salt / freshly ground black pepper
⅝ cup / 150 ml / ¼ pint hot chicken stock
2 tbs / 25 g / 1 oz butter
1 tbs brown sugar
1 tbs sherry

1 Grasp the flap of skin at the end of the bird and with the other hand, pull the skin away from the flesh as far as you can. Slide in sage leaves and cheese slices.

2 Place butter and onion in a bowl, cover and cook for 3 minutes. Mix in breadcrumbs, sage, seasoning and stock to form a moist, doughy consistency. Stuff the chicken and cook 8 – 10 minutes per 450 g / 1 lb.

3 Halfway through cooking time, place the butter, sugar and sherry in a small jug. Cook for 1 minute. Remove the bird from the oven and brush with the glaze. Return bird to oven, giving the dish a half turn, and complete cooking. Check to see if the chicken is done by sticking a skewer into it where the leg joins with the breast. The juices should run out clear.

4 Allow to stand for 15 minutes before serving.

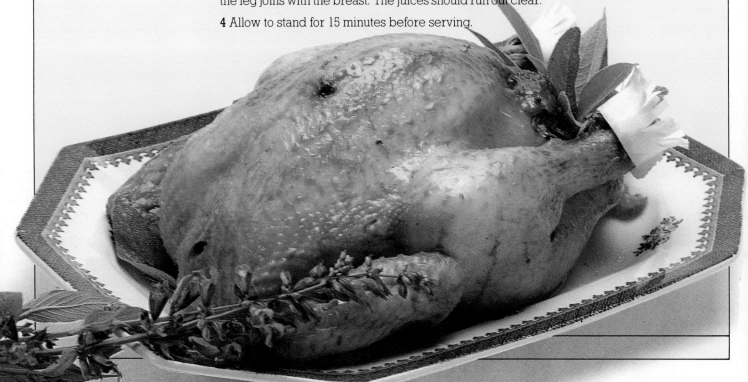

BEEF GOULASH

Serves 4 / Set: full and medium

5½ cups / 1 kg / 2 lb lean braising steak
½ cup / 2 oz / 50 g flour
½ tbs paprika
2 tbs oil
2 cloves garlic, crushed
1 tbs tomato paste
2 onions, sliced
2½ cups / 600 ml / 1 pint hot beef stock
1 bayleaf
200 g / 7 oz can tomatoes, mashed
4 tbs yoghurt
2 tbs parsley, chopped

1 Cut the meat into bite-sized cubes. Mix flour and paprika together and toss meat in mixture.

2 Heat a browning dish on full power according to manufacturer's instructions. Pour oil into dish and cook on full for 1 minute. Add beef and cook for 5 minutes on full, turning frequently to brown all sides.

3 Place meat in a casserole with garlic, tomato paste, onion, stock, bayleaf and tomatoes. Cover and cook on full for 45 minutes until beef is tender. Leave to stand for 5 minutes.

4 Spoon over yoghurt and serve garnished with parsley. The dish goes well with noodles or mashed potatoes.

SPICY MEATLOAF WITH TOMATO SAUCE

Serves 4 – 6 / Set: full
1 tbs oil
1 onion, chopped
1 clove garlic, chopped
1 cup / 225 g / 8 oz minced (ground) beef
½ cup / 100 g / 4 oz sausagemeat
½ cup / 100 g / 4 oz bacon, rinded and minced (ground)
1 cup / 50 g / 2 oz fresh brown breadcrumbs
½ tsp mixed spice
1 tsp dried thyme
3 bayleaves
salt / freshly ground black pepper
1 egg, beaten
Sauce
2 tbs / 25 g / 1 oz butter
1 onion, chopped
1 clove garlic, chopped
425 g / 15 oz can tomatoes
1 tbs tomato paste
1 tsp mixed herbs
salt / freshly ground black pepper

1 Pour oil into a bowl and cook for 2 minutes. Stir in onion and garlic and cook for 3 minutes.

2 Add minced (ground) beef and sausagemeat, bacon, breadcrumbs, spices, herbs and seasoning and mix well. Bind together with the beaten egg.

3 Press mixture into a deep oval pie dish and cook for 6 minutes. Wrap in foil to keep warm and leave to stand for 10 – 15 minutes. Remove foil and cook for 5 minutes. Turn out the loaf and keep warm.

4 To make the sauce, place the butter in a bowl and cook for 1 minute. Mix in the onion and garlic and cook for 3 minutes. Add the remaining ingredients and seasoning to taste. Cook for 4 minutes. Blend the sauce in a liquidiser. Re-heat for a further minute before serving with the meatloaf.

SHEPHERD'S PIE

Serves 4 / Set: full
1 onion, chopped
1 clove garlic, chopped
2 tomatoes, peeled and chopped
2 carrots, chopped
⅝ cup / 300 ml / ½ pint hot beef or chicken stock
1 tbs tomato paste
1 tbs Worcestershire sauce
1 bayleaf
1 tsp dried mixed herbs
salt / freshly ground black pepper
1 tbs fresh breadcrumbs
1½ cups / 350 g / 12 oz minced (ground) beef or lamb, cooked
3 cups / 450 g / 1 lb potato, cooked
2 tbs / 25 g / 1 oz butter
1 egg, beaten
parsley

1 Place vegetables in a large pie dish with the stock and cook for 5 minutes.

2 Stir in tomato paste, Worcestershire sauce, herbs, seasoning, breadcrumbs and meat. Mix thoroughly.

3 Mash the potato with the butter and beaten egg and place on top of the meat. Cook for 15 minutes and brown under the grill (broiler) before serving, garnished with parsley.

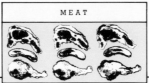

ARMENIAN LAMB WITH PILAFF

Serves 4 / Set: full
1 kg / 2 lb fillet end leg of lamb
1 tbs oil
2 tbs / 25 g / 1 oz butter
2 onions, chopped
1 clove garlic, chopped
4 tbs / 25 g / 1 oz flour
1 tsp ground cumin
½ tsp ground allspice
2 tbs tomato paste
⅝ cup / 300 ml/½ pint hot chicken stock
salt / freshly ground black pepper
Pilaff
3 tbs / 40 g / 1½ oz butter
1 small onion, chopped
1 cup / 250 g / 8 oz long-grain rice
1⅞ cups / 450 ml / ¾ pint hot chicken stock
salt / freshly ground black pepper
½ cup / 75 g / 3 oz currants
½ cup / 75 g / 3 oz almonds, blanched and chopped

1 Remove meat from bone and cut into bite-sized cubes.

2 Pour oil into a bowl, add butter and cook for 1 minute. Stir in onion and garlic and cook for 3 minutes. Add the meat and cook, covered, for 3 minutes.

3 Stir in the flour and add remaining ingredients. Cook, covered, for 10 minutes. Allow to stand for 15 mintues, then cook for a further 6 minutes.

4 To make the pilaff, place the butter in a large shallow dish and cook for 1 minute. Stir in onion and rice and cook for 4 minutes.

5 Add stock and seasoning and cook for 15 minutes or until rice is fluffy, adding extra stock if necessary. Check seasoning and stir in currants and almonds before serving with the lamb.

Armenian Lamb with Pilaff

MOUSSAKA

Serves 4 / Set: full
1 large aubergine (egg plant), sliced
salt
2 tbs / 25 g / 1 oz butter
2 onions, chopped
2 cloves garlic, chopped
2 cups / 100 g / 4 oz mushrooms, sliced
450 g / 1 lb lamb, minced (ground)
2 tbs tomato paste
1 tsp dried herbs
⅝ cup / 150 ml / ¼ pint hot beef stock
Sauce
2 tbs / 25 g / 1 oz butter
4 tbs / 25 g / 1 oz flour
⅝ cup / 300 ml / ½ pint milk
½ cup / 50 g / 2 oz Edam cheese, grated
1 egg, beaten
generous pinch of nutmeg

1 Sprinkle aubergine (egg plant) slices with salt and leave for 30 minutes. Rinse in cold water and pat dry with kitchen paper.

2 Place aubergine (egg plant) in a bowl, cover and cook for 3 minutes.

3 Place the butter, onions, garlic and mushrooms in a bowl. Cover and cook for 3 minutes.

4 Stir in the meat, tomato paste, herbs and stock. Cover and cook for 15 minutes.

5 For the sauce, place the butter in a jug and cook for 1 minute. Stir in the flour, then gradually blend in the milk. Cook for 3 minutes, stirring once.

6 Add the cheese, egg and nutmeg. Stir in well.

7 Layer the lamb and aubergine slices, onions, garlic and mushrooms alternately in a shallow casserole. Pour the sauce over and sprinkle with nutmeg. Cook for 10 minutes, turning the dish once. Serve.

VEAL WITH CREAM AND MUSHROOM SAUCE

Serves 4 / Set: full

450 g / 1 lb stewing veal, trimmed and diced
4 tbs / 25 g / 1 oz seasoned flour
4 tbs / 50 g / 2 oz butter
1 onion, chopped
1¾ cups / 100 g / 4 oz button mushrooms
⅝ cup / 300 ml / ½ pint dry white wine
⅝ cup / 300 ml / ½ pint hot chicken stock
1 tsp lemon juice
1 tsp dried sage
1 tbs cream
1 egg yolk
crispy bacon rolls
puff pastry crescents

1 Toss the veal in the flour. Place the butter in a large dish and cook for 1 minute. Stir in veal and cook for 6 minutes, stirring once.

2 Remove veal and place onion and mushrooms in the dish. Cook for 3 minutes.

3 Stir in the veal, wine, stock, lemon juice and sage and cook, covered, for 20 minutes.

4 Stir in the cream and egg yolk and serve garnished with crispy bacon rolls and puff pastry crescents.

Veal with Cream and Mushroom sauce

LIVER IN PORT AND ORANGE SAUCE

Serves 4 / Set: full
½ cup / 100 g / 4 oz butter
1 clove garlic, chopped
4 tbs orange juice
2 tbs parsley, chopped
750 g / 1½ lb lamb's or calf's liver, sliced
½ / 1 tbs cornflour (cornstarch)
4 tbs port
grated rind of 1 orange
salt / freshly ground black pepper

1 Place butter, garlic, orange juice and parsley in a bowl. Cover and cook for 3 minutes.

2 Add the liver slices, making sure they are well coated. Cover and cook for 7 – 10 minutes, until nearly done.

3 Blend the cornflour (cornstarch) with the port and orange rind and stir into the liver. Cook, uncovered, for 2 minutes, rearranging once. Serve with mashed potato and a green vegetable, such as spinach or broccoli.

VEGETABLES

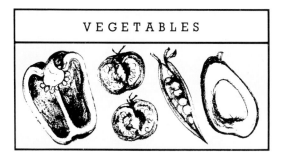

STUFFED PEPPERS

Serves 4 / Set: full
4 green, red or yellow peppers
½ cup / 100 g / 4 oz long-grain rice
1⅞ cups / 450 ml / ¾ pint hot beef stock
1 onion, finely chopped
1 clove garlic, finely chopped
salt / freshly ground black pepper
1 tsp dried mixed herbs
1 tbs tomato paste
⅓ cup / 50 g / 2 oz ham, finely chopped

1 Cut a slice from the top of each pepper and reserve to use as a lid. Remove core and seeds from peppers.

2 Place in a dish and cook for 5 – 6 minutes, turning once.

3 Place the rice, stock, onion, garlic, seasoning, herbs and tomato paste in a dish. Cover and cook for 10 minutes, or until stock is absorbed.

4 Stir the ham into the rice. Fill the peppers with the mixture and put on their lids. Return to the oven and cook for 4 minutes. Serve.

GREEN BEAN AND MUSHROOM CURRY

Serves 2 – 4 / Set: full
4 tbs / 50 g / 2 oz butter or ghee
1 large onion, chopped
2 cloves garlic, chopped
1 cup / 100 g / 4 oz green beans, trimmed and cut into 2 cm / 1 in lengths
2 cups / 100 g / 4 oz mushrooms, sliced
3 tomatoes, peeled and chopped
1 tbs lemon juice
2 slices fresh ginger
½ tsp turmeric
½ tsp ground coriander
½ tsp garam masala
fresh coriander or parsley

1 Place the butter or ghee in a bowl and cook for 1 minute. Add the onion and garlic and cook for 3 minutes.

2 Stir in the rest of the ingredients except the fresh coriander or parsley. Cover and cook for 15 minutes, stirring 3 times.

3 Garnish with fresh coriander or parsley and serve with brown rice (see page 00).

RUSSIAN BEETROOT

Serves 4 / Set: full
6 tbs / 75 g / 3 oz butter
5 medium uncooked beets, diced
2 tbs red wine vinegar
½ tsp dried dill
½ tsp dried fennel
salt / freshly ground black pepper
3 tbs / 25 g / 1 oz cornflower (cornstarch)
2 tbs milk
fresh dill or fennel
sour cream

1 Place butter in a bowl and cook for 1 minute. Stir in beets, vinegar, herbs and seasoning. Cover and cook for 8 minutes or until beets are tender.

2 Place cornflour (cornstarch) and milk in a small bowl and mix until smooth. Stir mixture into beets and cook, covered, for 4 – 6 minutes until thickened.

3 Allow to stand, covered, for 2 minutes. Garnish with fresh dill or fennel and serve hot or cold, with sour cream, to accompany cold meats.

SPINACH AND TOMATO QUICHE

Serves 6 / Set: full and medium
18 cm / 7 in pastry (pie) crust, cooked
450 g / 1 lb fresh spinach, washed and roughly chopped
1 onion, chopped
⅔ cup / 100 g / 4 oz cream cheese
2 large eggs, beaten
salt / freshly ground black pepper
1 large / 100 g / 4 oz tomato, peeled and chopped

1 Place spinach in a bowl and cook, covered, on full for 6 – 8 minutes until soft, stirring in onion halfway through cooking time.

2 Beat the cheese until smooth, then beat in the eggs and seasoning. Add the spinach, onion and tomatoes and mix thoroughly.

3 Turn the filling into the pastry case (pie shell). Cook on medium for 5 minutes. Allow to stand for 5 minutes. Cook on full for a further 8 minutes, or until filling has nearly set. Allow to stand for 5 minutes before serving.

TURNIP AND POTATO BAKE

Serves 4 / Set: full
2½ cups / 450 g / 1 lb turnips, peeled and thinly sliced
3 cups / 450 g / 1 lb potatoes, peeled and thinly sliced
butter
salt / freshly ground black pepper
4 tbs single (cereal) cream
chopped chives

1 Layer the turnips and potatoes in a round dish, dotting each layer with butter and seasoning with salt and pepper. Cover with waxed paper and press well down.

2 Stand the dish on an inverted plate. Cover and cook for 9 minutes, turning once.

3 Slowly pour over cream so that it seeps between the layers. Brown slightly under the grill (broiler), garnish with chives and serve.

RATATOUILLE ALLA MOZZARELLA

Serves 4 / Set: full
1 large aubergine (egg plant), sliced
3 courgettes (zucchini), sliced
4 tbs olive oil
1 large onion, sliced
2 cloves garlic, chopped
1 small red pepper, seeded and chopped
1 small green pepper, seeded and chopped
2 cups / 100 g / 4 oz mushrooms, sliced
425 g / 15 oz can tomatoes, mashed
1 tbs tomato paste
2 tsp fresh mixed herbs, chopped
1 bayleaf
salt / freshly ground black pepper
1 cup / 100 g / 4 oz mozzarella cheese, cubed

1 Place aubergine (egg plant) and courgettes (zucchini) in a colander, sprinkle with salt and allow to stand for 30 minutes. Rinse in cold water and pat dry. Cut the aubergine into bite-sized pieces.

2 Pour the oil into a casserole and cook for 1 minute. Add onion and garlic and cook for 1 minute. Stir in peppers, aubergine and courgettes and cook for 5 minutes, stirring once.

3 Stir in remaining ingredients, cover and cook for 15 minutes, stirring twice. Stir in mozzarella. Cover and cook for 5 minutes until cheese has melted. Serve with crusty French bread to mop up the juices.

AUSTRIAN RED CABBAGE

Serves 4 – 6 / Set: full
4 tbs / 50 g / 2 oz butter
1 large red cabbage, finely shredded
1 large onion, sliced
1 large cooking apple, diced
1 bayleaf
salt / freshly ground black pepper
2 tbs brown sugar
4 tbs red wine vinegar

1 Place butter in a large shallow dish and cook for 1 minute. Stir in cabbage and cook for 4 minutes.

2 Stir in remaining ingredients. Cover and cook for 25 minutes or until done. Serve as an accompaniment to roast pork.

PRAWN- OR SHRIMP-STUFFED TOMATOES

Serves 4 / Set: full
4 large Spanish tomatoes
2 tbs / 25 g / 1 oz butter
1 onion, finely chopped
1 clove garlic, finely chopped
1¼ cups / 150 g / 6 oz cooked peeled prawns or shrimps
1½ cups / 75 g / 3 oz fresh white breadcrumbs
2 tbs chopped parsley
2 tbs tomato paste
salt / freshly ground black pepper
lemon wedges

1 Cut the tops off the tomatoes, scoop out the pulp and reserve.

2 Place butter in a bowl and cook for 1 minute. Stir in onion and garlic. Cook for 2 minutes.

3 Stir in tomato pulp and rest of ingredients, except lemon wedges. Mix well. Stuff tomatoes and place upright in a shallow round dish. Cook, covered, for 5 minutes. Serve hot with lemon wedges.

BAKED POTATOES WITH SOUR CREAM AND CHIVES

Serves 1 / Set: full
1 large / 1 275 g / 10 oz potato
2 tbs sour cream
1 tsp chives, finely chopped
salt / freshly ground black pepper
crispy bacon bits

1 Scrub the potatoes and pat dry. Prick with a fork.

2 Cook for 12 minutes, or until soft.

3 Cut potato in half. Scoop out a spoonful of potato and mix with sour cream and chives. Season.

4 Return filling to potato, top with crispy bacon bits and cook for 1 minute.

BREAD, CAKES & BISCUITS

STRAWBERRY SHORTCAKE

Makes 8 pieces / Set: full
1½ cups / 175 g / 6 oz plain flour
⅓ cup / 50 g / 2 oz ground rice
pinch of salt
⅝ cup / 150 g / 5 oz butter
¼ cup / 50 g / 2 oz fine white sugar
⅝ cup / 150 ml / ¼ pint whipping cream, whipped
8 or more strawberries, sliced

1 Line a shallow 18 cm / 7 in dish with cling film (plastic wrap).

2 Place flour, ground rice and salt in a large bowl and mix well. Rub in the butter until the mixture is fine and crumbly.

3 Stir in the sugar and knead into a dough. Press the mixture into the dish and smooth down with a palette knife. Mark into 8 pieces and prick all over with a fork.

4 Cook for 4 mintues, giving the dish a quarter turn each minute.

5 Sprinkle with sugar, cool slightly and cut into 8. Allow to cool completely on a wire rack.

6 Decorate with piped whipped cream and sliced strawberries.

FLAPJACKS

Makes 12 flapjacks / Set: full
6 tbs / 75 g / 3 oz butter
3 tbs golden syrup
1⅓ cups / 100 g / 4 oz porridge oats
2 tbs / 25 g / 1 oz brown sugar
¼ cup / 25 g / 1 oz mixed peel

1 Line a shallow 20 cm × 25 cm / 8 in × 10 in rectangular dish with cling film (plastic wrap).

2 Place butter and syrup in a bowl and cook for 1 minute. Stir in oats, sugar and peel, mixing thoroughly. Press mixture into base of dish and mark into 12.

3 Cook for 3 minutes, turning once. Cool slightly, cut into 12 and allow to cool completely on a wire rack.

Flapjacks

GINGERBREAD

Serves 6 – 10 / Set: full
8 tbs black treacle (molasses)
⅜ cup / 75 g / 3 oz brown sugar
½ cup / 100 g / 4 oz butter
1 cup / 100 g / 4 oz self-raising flour
1 cup / 100 g / 4 oz wholemeal flour
½ tsp bicarbonate of soda
1 tsp ground ginger
1 tsp mixed spice
2 eggs, beaten

1 Place the treacle (molasses), sugar and butter in a bowl and cook for 2 minutes. Allow to stand for 2 minutes.

2 Stir in the flour, bicarbonate of soda and spices. Beat in the eggs.

3 Grease a deep oblong dish and pour in the mixture. Stand on an upturned plate and cook for 4 minutes, turning twice.

4 Allow to stand for 5 minutes before turning out onto a wire rack to cool completely. Serve cut into slices and buttered.

CHOCOLATE AND HAZELNUT CAKE

Serves 10 / Set: full
100 g / 4 oz cup molasses
½ cup / 100 g / 4 oz butter
1½ cups / 175 g / 6 oz self-raising or plain flour with ¾ tsp baking powder added
6 tbs / 50 g / 2 oz cocoa powder
½ cup / 100 g / 4 oz brown sugar
¼ cup / 50 g / 2 oz hazelnuts, chopped
2 eggs, beaten
1 tsp vanilla essence (extract)
⅝ cup / 150 ml / ¼ pint single (cereal) cream
Decoration
⅝ cup / 150 ml / ¼ pint whipping cream, whipped
chocolate flake

1 Line a 19 cm / 7½ in round dish with greased waxed paper.

2 Rub the molasses and butter into the flour and cocoa. Stir in the sugar and hazelnuts. Beat in the other ingredients and spread mixture evenly in dish.

3 Cook for 6 minutes, giving dish a half turn half-way through cooking time. Allow to cool for 10 minutes before turning out onto a wire rack to cool completely.

4 Decorate with rosettes of cream and chocolate flake.

FRUIT CAKE

Serves 10 / Set: full
½ cup / 100 g / 4 oz butter
2 eggs, beaten
pinch of salt
½ cup / 100 g / 4 oz brown sugar
2 tbs black treacle (molasses)
1½ cups / 175 g / 6 oz plain flour with ¾ tsp baking powder added
¼ cup / 25 g / 1 oz mixed peel
¼ cup / 25 g / 1 oz glacé cherries, chopped
2 tbs / 25 g / 1 oz sultanas
2 tbs / 25 g / 1 oz nuts, chopped
1 tbs lemon juice

1 Grease a 1.5 litre / 2¾ pint round dish and line the bottom with greased waxed paper. Turn the mixture into the dish and cook for 5 – 7 minutes.

2 Place butter in a bowl and cook for 1 minute.

3 Add eggs, salt, sugar and treacle, mixing well. Fold in flour. Mix in remaining ingredients.

4 Allow to stand for 10 minutes before turning out onto a wire rack to cool.

ORANGE SPONGE CAKE

Serves 10 / Set: full
2¼ cups / 250 g / 8 oz plain flour with 1 tsp baking powder added
baking powder
½ cup / 100 g / 4 oz butter
½ cup / 100 g / 4 oz brown sugar
2 eggs
2 tbs orange juice
grated rind of half an orange
1 cup / 50 g / 2 oz candied peel
1⅔ cups / 225 g / 8 oz icing sugar
2 tbs water
orange food colouring
sugared orange slices

1 Spoon sponge mixture into prepared container. Stand on an upturned plate and cook for 5 minutes, turning container twice.

2 Sift flour and baking powder into a mixing bowl. Rub in butter until mixture is crumbly. Mix in sugar.

3 Make a well in the mixture and break the eggs into it. Gradually beat the eggs into the mixture. Stir in orange juice, orange rind and candied peel.

4 Line a straight-sided 18 cm / 7 in round, 9 cm / 3½ in deep container with greased waxed paper.

5 Allow to stand for 5 minutes before turning onto a wire rack to cool completely.

6 Mix icing sugar with water and add orange food colouring. Coat cake with icing and decorate with sugared orange slices.

VICTORIA SANDWICH

Serves about 8 / Set: full
¾ cup / 175 g / 6 oz butter
¾ cup / 175 g / 6 oz fine white sugar
3 eggs, beaten
1½ cup / 175 g / 6 oz plain flour with ¾ tsp baking powder added
pinch of salt
about 2 tbs warm milk
5 tbs strawberry jam
⅝ cup / 150 ml / ½ pint whipping cream, whipped
icing sugar

1 Line a 20 cm / 8 in cake or soufflé dish with cling film (plastic wrap).

2 Cream the butter with the sugar until soft and light. Gradually beat in the eggs. Sift the flour with the salt and fold into the mixture a third at a time, adding enough milk to make the mixture drop easily from the spoon.

3 Spoon mixture into the dish and cook for 6 – 8 minutes, giving the dish a half turn every 2 minutes. The cake is done when a wooden cocktail stick or toothpick inserted in the top comes out clean. It may be moist on top, but this will dry out. Allow to stand for 5 minutes before lifting out and cooling completely on a wire rack.

4 When cool, carefully slice the cake in half horizontally. Spread the base with jam, spread over the whipped cream and sandwich the two halves together. Dredge with icing sugar.

WHITE BREAD

Makes a 1 kg / 2 lb loaf / Set: full
1 tsp sugar
⅝ cup / 300 ml / ½ pint warm water
1 tsp dried yeast
4½ cups / 450 g / 1 lb plain flour
½ tsp salt
3 tbs / 40 g / 1½ oz butter
2 tsp oil
1 tbs poppy seeds

1 Grease a 1 kg / 2 lb loaf or soufflé dish and line the bottom with waxed paper.

2 Place sugar in a jug and add half the water. Cook for 30 seconds. Stir in the yeast and allow to stand for 10 – 15 minutes.

3 Sift flour and salt into a bowl and cook for 30 seconds. Rub in the butter. Make a well in the middle of the flour and gradually add the sugared water and yeast, stirring. Add as much of the remaining water as necessary to make a soft dough. Knead on a floured board until dough is elastic.

4 Place dough in a floured bowl and cover with cling film (plastic wrap). Cook for 15 seconds to prove. Leave to stand in a warm place until the dough has risen to double its size, giving occasional 5 second blasts in the oven if liked.

6 Turn out dough and knead well for a further 2 – 3 minutes. Shape and place in loaf dish. Cover with a clean damp tea towel and leave in a warm place until doubled in size.

7 Oil the top of the loaf and sprinkle with poppy seeds. Cook for 5 minutes, turning once. Allow to stand for 10 minutes. Turn out onto a wire cooling rack and allow to cool completely.

8 Brown crust under the grill (broiler) if liked.

WHOLEWHEAT ROLLS

Makes 16 / Set: full
⅝ cup / 300 ml / ½ pint milk
2 tsp dried yeast
1 tsp fine white sugar
4½ cups / 450 g / 1 lb wholewheat flour
1 tsp salt
2 tsp malt extract
2 tsb oil
1 egg, beaten
2 tbs poppy seeds

1 Pour milk into a jug and cook for half a minute. Stir in the yeast and sugar. Allow to stand for 15 minutes, stirring occasionally, until frothy.

2 Sift flour and salt into a large bowl. Cook for half a minute.

3 Stir in the yeast mixture, malt extract and oil. If necessary, add more milk to make a pliable dough. Knead until dough loses its stickiness. Leave in a floured bowl covered with cling film (plastic wrap) in a warm place until dough has risen to twice its size.

4 Knead lightly, divide into 16 and shape into rolls. Place on a floured tray, cover with a damp tea towel and leave in a warm place to rise for a further 20 minutes.

5 Brush with beaten egg and sprinkle with poppy seeds. Place on a sheet of greased waxed paper and bake in two batches for 3 – 4 minutes, turning once.

6 Allow to cool on a wire rack. For a crisper, browner crust, brown under the grill (broiler) for a few minutes.

PUDDINGS AND DESSERTS

FRUIT SPONGE PUDDING

Serves 6 / Set: full
2 tbs jam or syrup
½ cup / 100 g / 4 oz butter
½ cup / 100 g / 4 oz fine white sugar
2 eggs
1 cup / 100 g / 4 oz self-raising flour (or plain flour with 1 tsp baking powder added to it)
½ cup / 50 g / 4 oz glacé cherries, chopped
⅜ cup / 50 g / 2 oz dried apricots, chopped
⅓ cup / 50 g / 2 oz sultanas
½ tsp baking powder
2 tbs water

1 Grease a 1 litre / 1¾ pint pudding basin (or 1 large baking dish). Place jam or syrup in the bottom of it.

2 Place the butter, sugar, eggs and flour in a bowl and beat together for 1 minute. Stir in fruit, baking powder into basin on top of jam. Cover with cling film (plastic wrap) and slit in 2 or 3 places. Cook for 6 minutes.

3 Allow to stand for 3 minutes, turn out and serve.

PINEAPPLE UPSIDE-DOWN PUDDING

Serves 4 – 6 / Set: medium and full
2 tbs / 25 g / 1 oz butter
¼ cup / 50 g / 2 oz demerara sugar
6 pineapple rings
6 glacé cherries
½ cup / 100 g / 4 oz margarine
½ cup / 100 g / 4 oz fine white sugar
2 eggs
1 cup / 100 g / 4 oz plain flour, with ½ tsp baking powder added
a little milk

1 Put the butter and demerara sugar in a 4 cm / 2 in deep, 20 cm / 8 in round dish and cook on full for 2 minutes until melted. Make sure syrup covers bottom of dish.

2 Drain pineapple rings and reserve the juice. Arrange the pineapple rings and cherries in a pattern on the bottom of the dish.

3 In a mixing bowl, cream together the margarine and sugar. Beat the eggs with a balloon whisk until fluffy, then beat the eggs and flour into the sugar and margarine a little at a time. Mix to a soft dropping consistency with pineapple juice or milk.

4 Spread the sponge mixture over the pineapple base and cook on medium for 10 minutes, then on full for 2 minutes until the sponge is set. Allow to cool slightly, and when sponge has shrunk away from the sides of the dish, turn out onto a plate.

BREAD AND BUTTER PUDDING

Serves 4 / Set: medium
6 slices white bread, crusts removed
6 tbs / 75 g / 3 oz butter
⅓ cup / 50 g / 2 oz raisins
1⅞ cup / 450 ml / ¾ pint milk
3 eggs, beaten
3 eggs, beaten
2 tbs / 40 g / 1½ oz sugar
1 tsp nutmeg

1 Grease a 1.25 litre / 2 pint pie dish (quart plate). Spread the bread with butter and cut the slices in half diagonally. Arrange bread with sultanas in dish.

2 Beat together the milk and eggs and stir in the sugar. Pour over the bread and cook for 25 – 28 minutes, pressing bread well down into custard.

3 Allow to stand for 5 minutes, sprinkle with sugar and nutmeg and brown under the grill (broiler) before serving.

CHRISTMAS PUDDING

Makes 2 600 ml / 1 pint puddings / Set: full
1 cup / 100 g / 4 oz plain flour
pinch of salt
1 tbs mixed spice
2 cups / 100 g / 4 oz breadcrumbs
½ cup / 100 g / 4 oz brown sugar
½ cup / 100 g / 4 oz suet
1 cup / 175 g / 6 oz sultanas
1⅓ cups / 225 g / 8 oz seedless raisins
½ cup / 50 g / 2 oz candied peel
grated rind of 1 orange
1 eating apple, peeled and grated
juice of 1 lemon
2 eggs, beaten
3 tbs black treacle (molasses)
⅝ cup / 150 ml / ¼ pint stout

1 Grease 2 600 ml / 1 pint pudding basins (or 2 large baking dishes).

2 Place all the dry ingredients in a bowl and mix well. Stir in remaining ingredients.

3 Divide the mixture between the basins. Cover with cling film (plastic wrap) and slit in 2 or 3 places.

4 Cook each pudding for 5 minutes. Allow to stand for 10 minutes before turning out.

CHOCOLATE CHEESECAKE

Serves 8 / Set: full
3 cups / 175 g / 6 oz digestive biscuits
4 tbs / 50 g / 2 oz butter
1 tbs brandy
1 cup / 100 g / 4 oz plain chocolate, broken up into small pieces
¼ cup / 50 g / 2 oz fine white sugar
1⅓ cups / 250 g / 8 oz cream cheese
1¼ cups / 300 ml / ½ pint whipping cream
2 eggs, separated
crystallised flowers and leaves

1 Line a 23 cm / 9 in flan dish (pie plate) with cling film (plastic wrap).

2 Place digestive biscuits in a plastic bag and crush with a rolling pin.

3 Place butter in a bowl and cook for 1 minute. Add crushed biscuits and mix well. Press into bottom of flan dish, and sprinkle with brandy.

4 Place chocolate in a bowl with a little water and cook for 3 minutes or until melted. Stir in sugar. Gradually beat in cream cheese, half the cream and the egg yolks.

5 Whisk egg whites until stiff and fold into mixture. Pour into dish on top of biscuit crust. Cook for 8 minutes. Allow to cool.

6 For the topping, whip the remaining cream and pipe round the edge. Decorate with crystallised flowers and leaves.

LEMON CHEESECAKE

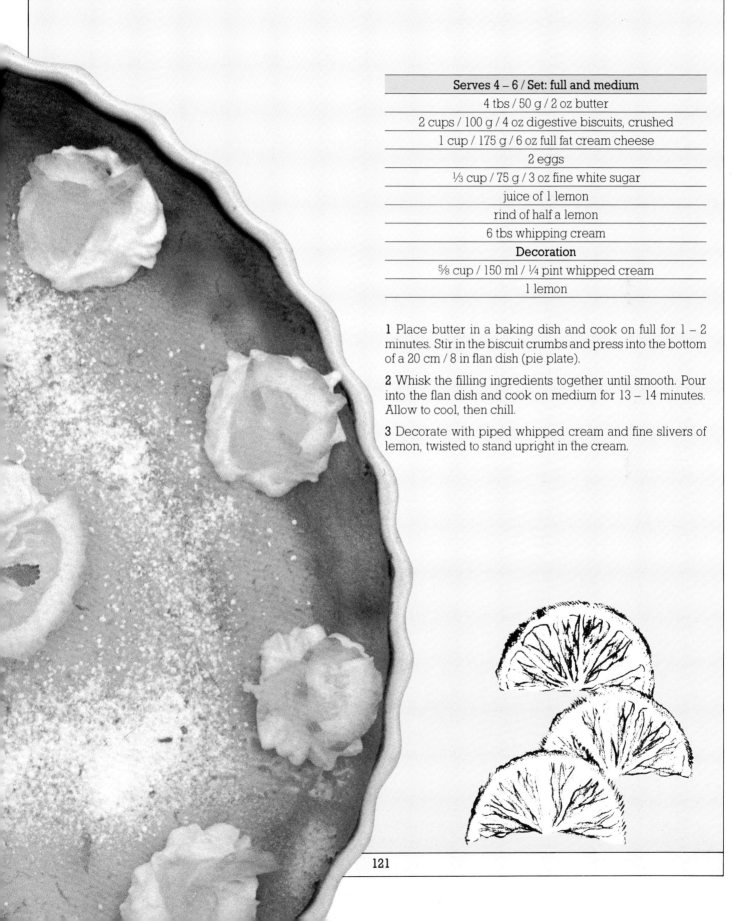

Serves 4 – 6 / Set: full and medium
4 tbs / 50 g / 2 oz butter
2 cups / 100 g / 4 oz digestive biscuits, crushed
1 cup / 175 g / 6 oz full fat cream cheese
2 eggs
⅓ cup / 75 g / 3 oz fine white sugar
juice of 1 lemon
rind of half a lemon
6 tbs whipping cream
Decoration
⅝ cup / 150 ml / ¼ pint whipped cream
1 lemon

1 Place butter in a baking dish and cook on full for 1 – 2 minutes. Stir in the biscuit crumbs and press into the bottom of a 20 cm / 8 in flan dish (pie plate).

2 Whisk the filling ingredients together until smooth. Pour into the flan dish and cook on medium for 13 – 14 minutes. Allow to cool, then chill.

3 Decorate with piped whipped cream and fine slivers of lemon, twisted to stand upright in the cream.

BAKED STUFFED PEARS

Serves 4 / Set: full
4 pears, cored
2 tbs / 25 g / 1 oz butter
2 tbs / 25 g / 1 oz brown sugar
2 tbs / 25 g / 1 oz raisins or sultanas
3 tbs hot water
2 tbs honey

1 Place pears in a shallow dish.

2 Place butter, sugar and fruit in a bowl and mix well. Press stuffing into pears.

3 Mix water and honey together and spoon over pears. Cook for 9 minutes or until pears are tender.

CARAMELISED ORANGES

Serves 4 / Set: full
4 large juicy oranges
¾ cup / 175 g / 6 oz fine white sugar
6 tbs water

1 Peel the oranges, removing all the pith. Slice, and remove pips. Arrange in a serving dish.

2 Place the sugar and water in a bowl and cook for 10 – 20 minutes until golden brown. Pour the caramel over the oranges.

3 Chill overnight and serve with whipped cream and brandy snaps.

APPLE, DATE AND WALNUT CRUMBLE

Serves 4 / Set: full
about 6 large apples / 900 g / 2 lb cooking apples, peeled, cored and sliced
½ cup / 75 g / 3 oz dates, chopped
½ cup / 50 g / 2 oz walnuts, chopped
2 cloves
pinch of cinnamon
½ cup / 100 g / 4 oz fine white sugar
1½ cups / 150 g / 6 oz white flour
75 g / 6 oz butter
50 g / 2 oz brown sugar

1 Place the fruit and nuts in a pie dish with the cloves and cinnamon. Sprinkle over the sugar.

2 Sift the flour into a bowl and rub in the butter till crumbly. Stir in most of the brown sugar.

3 Top the fruit with the crumble and sprinkle over the remaining brown sugar. Cook for 12 – 14 minutes, turning once.

RASPBERRY SOUFFLE

Serves 6 / Set: full
2 tbs kirsch
4 tbs water
2 tbs powdered gelatine
1¼ cups / 300 ml / ½ pint liquidised raspberries
½ cup / 100 g / 4 oz fine white sugar
1¼ cups / 300 ml / ½ pint cream, whipped
6 egg whites, stiffly whipped
Decoration
1¼ cups / 300 ml / ½ pint whipping cream, stiffly whipped
12 raspberries

1 Place the kirsch and water in a bowl and stir in the gelatine. Cook for 30 seconds until gelatine has dissolved. Stir well.

2 Mix in the raspberry purée and sugar and allow to cool, stirring occasionally.

3 Fold in the cream with a small spatula, then fold in the egg whites.

4 Spoon the mixture into a soufflé dish and chill until set. Decorate with piped whipped cream and raspberries.

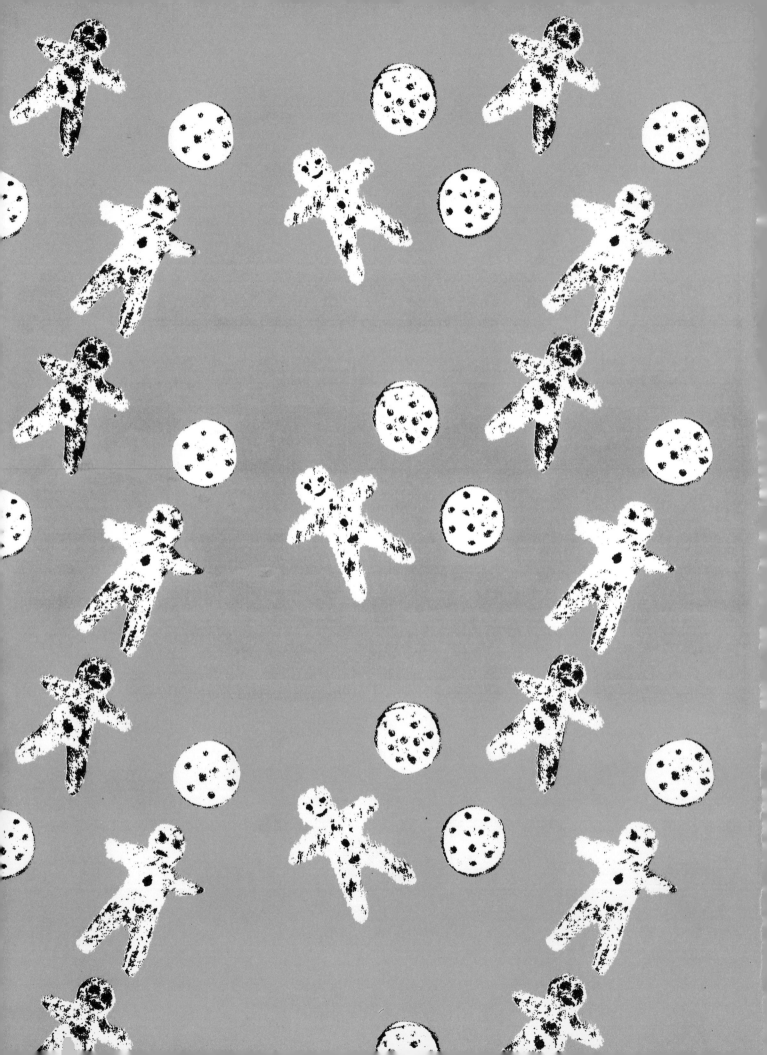